The Plant-Based Vegan Diet for Bodybuilding Athletes

Healthy Muscle, Vitality, High Protein, and Energy for the Rest of your Life. Everything You Need To Know About Basing Your Diet On A Plant Solution

Pete Bondy

1

Furthermore, the information that can be found within the pages described forthwith shall be considered both accurate and truthful when it comes to the recounting of facts. As such, any use, correct or incorrect, of the provided information will render the Publisher free of responsibility as to the actions taken outside of their direct purview. Regardless, there are zero scenarios where the original author or the Publisher can be deemed liable in any fashion for any damages or hardships that may result from any of the information discussed herein.

Additionally, the information in the following pages is intended only for informational purposes and should thus be thought of as universal. As befitting its nature, it is presented without assurance regarding its prolonged validity or interim quality. Trademarks that are mentioned are done without written consent and can in no way be considered an endorsement from the trademark holder.

Introduction

I would like to thank you for choosing *The Plant-Based Vegan Diet for Bodybuilding Athletes*. The information ahead is meant to help you make the switch to a vegan diet.

Following a plant-based diet has become very popular over the past decade. People switch for ethical and health reasons, and it is a great diet for people who are serious about getting healthy. But the one group of people that are still strongly judged about begin vegans are bodybuilders.

It has been a belief that the only way a person can gain muscle is by eating a bunch of lean poultry, dairy, and eggs. But the fact of the matter is, you can eat vegan and still gain muscle, and that's what this book is going to show you.

We will go over why a vegan diet is such a great idea for bodybuilders, beside the obvious health benefits. You will also learn why all of those "beliefs" about veganism and bodybuilding are wrong.

Then we'll get into what it means to eat clean. I'm sure you've heard that everybody should eat clean, but oftentimes people don't know what it means to eat clean. Then we'll move into vitality and energy. This is the biggest worry bodybuilders tend to have about following a plant-based diet, but I'll make sure you know exactly what to do to make sure you maintain your energy.

Then we'll move into picking the right foods and making sure that you get the calories and protein you need. Protein is probably the most important part for everybody on a plant-based diet. Then we'll discuss gut health. This is something that people tend to forget about, but gut health is a very important part of your overall health.

Then we will jump into those pieces of advice that are sure to prevent the gains they promise. There is a lot of bodybuilding advice out there that has been around for years, but it isn't helpful in the least. Unlearning that advice is one of the best things you can do.

Then we will look at your pre and post-workout nutrition to make sure that you get the most out of your workouts. This is often where people get nervous about a plant-based diet, but there are plenty of plant-based foods that can give you the energy you need for your workout, and help your muscles recover afterward.

Then we will look at the vegan supplements you should consider taking. While there are a lot of foods out there that can give you the nutrients you need, most vegans do need supplements to fill the gaps, and this is especially true for bodybuilders.

Then we'll round things out by look at foods that will boost your anabolic functions your body. These are foods that will help you to gain muscle and basically work as natural and legal steroids.

Let's not waste anymore time, let's get into what you really came here for.

Chapter 1:Simple Nutrition Equals More Muscles

If you were a plant-based bodybuilder a decade ago, you would have been seen as an oxymoron. For a long time now, all we have heard is that in order to build muscles, you have to eat a lot of meat. The times are changing, and bodybuilders now realize that they don't want to consume as many animal products.

It's obvious that a plant-based diet can provide you with lots of health benefits. People who follow a plant-based diet have a lower risk of obesity than the national average. Considering that there is research that says processed and red meat can shorten a person's life expectancies, plant-based dieters tend to live longer.

But, there is still concern among bodybuilders about the ability to increase or maintain their size and strength. I want to assure you that when you start taking into account the attention and planning that you put into your lifestyle, you will quickly realize that being a vegan bodybuilder isn't all that much harder to follow than the diet you are following right now.

There are bodybuilding nutrition facts that remain true even if you are following a plant-based diet. The truth is, all you are doing is adapting what you have already learned about building muscle and getting rid of fat and turning it plant-based. You are simply making your nutrition simpler.

There are few important pieces of information to take into consideration when you switch to a plant-based diet as a bodybuilder. This includes making sure you get enough protein, you keep your carbs balanced, along with plenty of vitamin B12, EPA, and DHA.

Busting the Myth

The stereotype of the plant-based dieter isn't all that flattering. They are seen as people who are always tired, super thin, gaunt with barely any nutrient left in their body, and just enough protein in their bodies to help them stand. Let's not even get into the idea of them being about to gain muscle tissue. This isn't a pleasant image at all, but it is also at all accurate.

The truth is whole-food plant-based dieters that make sure they eat a large range of foods, like whole grains, legumes, beans, seeds, nuts, fruits, and vegetables, can enjoy a healthy nutrient profile, moreso than people who consume the standard American diet. For the vegans that make sure that they eat the right types of plant-based foods, they are less likely to suffer nutrient problems.

But, people are still saying, "What about protein?"

Plant-based dieters do tend to consume less protein than people who eat meat. But does this validate the stereotypes of vegans? No, because whether you eat meat or not, there is still a good chance that you will be consuming around twice the daily amount of protein you need.

You have the choice of eating everything from beans and lentils to soy-based foods and all of those wonderful vegan meat products on the market now. Beyond Meat's Beyond Burger contains more protein than your regular beef burger with 20 grams a patty. Also, there is the fact that we believe we need way more protein to function than we actually do. If you want numbers for how much protein you need as a bodybuilder, you should aim for 0.36 to 0.86 grams of protein per pound. And before you say, "Well, I might eat a bit more because you can never have too much protein," you may want to reconsider. There are studies that show consuming more than your recommended daily need of protein could increase your risk of kidney disease and osteoporosis, no matter where you get your protein.

While meat-eaters may get a few extra grams every day, even the strictest vegans will end up eating more protein than they actually need. By the way, too much animal protein has been connected to serious chronic diseases. It's also important to know that while the public believes plant proteins are inferior to animal proteins, there has been research they have found that plant protein has the same amino acids as dairy and meat. If you are making sure you are building your meals around a wide variety of plant-based foods, you will be consuming enough usable protein.

Of course, when we're talking about bodybuilding, there are some people who have the mindset that enough isn't enough. Is a vegan bodybuilder really going to be able to get enough nutrients to push their muscles to extremes?

Nutrients

Besides worries about proteins, the next thing people worry about is becoming deficient in minerals and vitamins. While everybody needs to make sure that they are getting the nutrients they need, those who actively build muscle need to worry just a bit more to make sure their body is getting everything it needs.

A vitamin B12 deficiency is the most common deficiency a vegan will face, but not all vegans will suffer from this. Anybody, no matter what diet they follow, are at a risk of developing a vitamin B12 deficiency if they don't follow a balanced diet. Some of the most common signs are balance problems, confusion, depression, and fatigue.

To make sure that you are getting enough B12, you should eat things like mushrooms, nutritional yeast, and fortified cereals.

calories you consume. It won't take you that long for you to figure out how much food you are going to have to eat to get the gains you want.

So, yes, it is entirely possible to be successful at bodybuilding while also following a plant-based diet. For example, the Italian bodybuilder Massimo Brunaccioni is vegan, and it hasn't held him back at all. He even placed second in the 2018 World Natural Bodybuilding Federation

What You May Not Know

For people new to a plant-based diet, they often don't realize that many grains, legumes, and vegetables have decent levels of protein. For example, beans have a lot of protein as well as slow-digesting fiber and carbs. Lentils contain 27% protein by calorie. A cup of lentils has 63% of your fiber requirements. Then you have your leafy vegetables. On average, leafy vegetables contain 40% protein by calorie, and they are full of micronutrients. A bunch of kale has 12 grams of protein. While this may not seem like a lot of protein for a single meal, if you look at it over the course of a day or multiple protein sources in a single meal, those amounts will add up. Then you have things like nutritional yeast that contains six grams of protein in two tablespoons, and everybody loves peanut butter, and that contains six grams of protein in two tablespoons.

And just like carnivorous bodybuilders, you can feel free to add in a protein shake or two during your day if you aren't reaching your protein needs.

Living Proof

If you're still not sold on a simple plant-based diet being right for bodybuilders than I have some proof for you. We're going to take a look at Jon Venus. He is a bodybuilder, Youtuber, and trainer, who has been vegan for a few years now. He made the switch after he learned about the environmental implications animal farming has on the world.

Venus has stated that he was surprised by the improvements he experienced in the gym after he went 100% plant-based. His first noticeable improvement was his energy levels, and he noticed that he wasn't as sore after a workout. That was just during his first three months of being vegan. He also says that you have to know what your goals are so that you can eat foods that will help you to reach them.

He suggests to his clients, whether they are vegan or not, that they keep a macro ratio around 60% of your calories coming from carbs, 20% fat, and 20% protein. And he consumes around 80 to 180 grams of protein every day.

Chapter 2:Clean Eating

One of the most popular terms that you will hear in terms of nutrition is also one of the most confusing. Let's take a moment to look at what clean really means when it comes to clean eating. I'll admit it; I don't really like it when I hear people saying that you need to "eat clean." While this phrase has been around for a long time now, it has only been recently that it grew in popularity. This was due to a more vocal fitness community who stuck their noses up while preaching about different and conflicting things. You would think that two little words would have a clear definition, but it doesn't.

So what's the problem I have with those words? Despite the fact that it is popular among books, diet plans, blogs, magazines, and so on, there isn't a single definition of what "clean" means. It's hard to know what a person means when they mention it. Plus, I don't know what they're eating or how effective it is going to be whatever goals they may have.

That doesn't mean some of the definitions aren't good. Sometimes "clean" is used in a way that makes sense, but there are others who define it in a way that it would only help them with their goals. We're going to go through this clean eating journey together and figure out what it means in a useful sense so that you can move forward and be a cleaning eating, plant-based bodybuilder.

Processed Foods

One of the most popular pieces of advice you will receive about clean eating says that if it's processed, it can't be clean. Basically, if something comes prepackaged and is located within those horrible "middle aisles" of the grocery store, then you should run far and fast away from it. Most clean eating people will slap those boxes right out of your hand.

But, I have a problem with this part of clean eating. It isn't sustainable to try to completely eliminate processed foods. Unless you are living on a self-sustaining farm or you are a true hunter-gatherer, this isn't going to be possible. The other 99% of the population who isn't tending to out asparagus garden is going to be consuming some form of processed food.

There are some people who would refer to this as eating "real" food or trying to keep things "as close to nature" as they can. They say that they only eat foods that are in season. In my book, this just causes a simple diet to become a real pain. If its winter and I'm cold, I am going to want to have soup. Sometimes I'm not going to be able to plan ahead and have all of the ingredients I need so that I can soak the beans overnight. If I followed this particular principle perfectly, I would be able to eat canned soups. That means if there is a day when I don't feel like cooking and waiting, I would either go hungry or eat something that I'm not in the mood for.

Processing foods isn't all that bad, and it often improve its safety and bioavailability of some antioxidants and nutrients. It also gives you the chance to quickly fix all of the lovely and delicious dishes on Instagram and Pinterest.

Plus, there are plenty of healthy processed foods out there, such as hummus, whole-grain cereal, tomato sauce. Nutrition is a very complex subject, and sure it might be easier if we could just wipe out complete categories of food, but all this does is hurt your taste buds, wallet, and time.

Unrefined Grains

Unlike the processed food advice, the people who say unrefined grains are better than refined grains are right. Whole grains are a great way to consume fiber, and they have a lot of B vitamins. Refined grains get around 20 various nutrients taken out of them, but then most of them added back in during processing. But there is a caveat; there are a lot of grains that don't add back the important nutrients. If at all possible, go with the unrefined grains to make sure you get all of the nutrients they have to offer.

Eat All Macros

Some will preach that you have to eat every macro and every meal you have. Research has said that it is important that adults eat around 25 to 30 grams of protein with every meal in order to build and maintain muscles. As a bodybuilder, you should prioritize protein. Fat is also said to be important so that you are able to absorb fat-soluble vitamins, so it's a good idea to have a bit of fat with your meal when you eating leafy greens or taking a multivitamin. And we also know that some high-fiber carbs help to make the bacteria in the gut happy and healthy.

You can feel free to make sure that every single meal contains all of the macronutrients. However, it's not necessarily essential to scurry around looking for your olives or whole grains to complement what you are eating. Sometimes, a protein shake is perfectly acceptable, and the same is true for a handful of olives, some fruit, or a simple salad.

Eliminate or Cut Down Sugars

There are some who even include fat and salt into this, but I won't get into how this is such an outdated way of thinking. Foods that have added sugars are pretty much useless, especially for non-athletes. If you are a bodybuilder training for competition, then some added sugars aren't going to hurt you. Sugars, when added to foods in order to make them more palatable, as opposed to the sugars that come natural in some foods, only add calories with no real health benefits.

So cutting back on added sugars is a good idea when it comes to clean eating. But what kind of difference can it make? There was a study published by Cornell University where they study the foods in 500 homes in Syracuse, New York, and what the body compositions of the inhabitants were. The ones who had breakfast cereals ended up weighing 20 pounds more than the people who didn't People with soft drinks weighted 24 to 26 pounds more. People who had a fruit bowl weighed 13 pounds.

Sure, you can have the occasional pastry if you want to, but for those who want to "clean up" their eating, then cutting back on added sugars is a great idea.

So if you were to ask five health coaches, personal trainers, or dietitians what it means to eat clean, you are going to get just as many responses. There may be a few similar concepts, but there won't be a lot to do with "clean" foods. While I think eating clean is a good idea, if done correctly, you should be wary of anybody preaching about "clean." Oftentimes, it is just going to end up costing you a lot of money and will end up making you feel frustrated. Plus, it may not even improve your nutrition.

On the other hand, if you follow the rules, I'm going to go over with you and keep a reasonable approach, such as cutting back on added sugars and portion sizes, you will be surprised how great you will feel.

How to Really Eat Clean

Getting clean shouldn't require a huge overhaul to your diet, especially if you are switching to a plant-based diet. If you go at it that way, then you are probably going about it wrong. Here are some things to keep in mind when getting clean.

1. Look at the nutrients, and not just the calories.

Don't allow yourself to get caught up in the numbers. When it comes to our bodyweight-conscious world, it's very easy to get caught in the numbers game. While it might work well for a person looking to lose weight, it isn't going to actually make them healthy.

The calorie-counting diet dates back to the 70s and 80s and is a thing of the past. It is much more important that you get all of the nutrients you need to than to focus on your overall calorie balance. Look at it this way; one way will make you feel grumpy and guilty when you do eat. The other gives you energy, stabilizes your blood sugar, and you will discover foods you never knew existed.

2. Move past refined white flours.

You can cut out the refined white flours you use for baking, and bake some things with unrefined flours and other flour substitutes. It could mean that you have to try out some new recipes and make some mistakes, but it is doable. Besides looking for unrefined wheat flours, you can also try out oat, brown rice, coconut, and almond flour. Using those choices will help to lower your carbohydrate intake, and you can still make delicious dishes with them.

These various flours also come with different nutritional profiles, so you will want to read on them to see which one fits your dietary needs the most.

3. Balance out your diet.

The two main ideas of clean eating are moderation and balance. You shouldn't avoid dietary fats and carbs completely, or you are going to end up dreading mealtimes. Make sure you eat them, but simply adjust your portion sizes so that it fits into your goals and nutrient needs.

Depending on your system needs, your macro ratio could end up being broken down into several different ways. If you lean more towards unsaturated fats and complex carbohydrates, then you are on the right track. What it all boils down to is to make sure that you are mindful of the foods you eat. You have a problem when you don't know what you are consuming.

4. Sit down to your meals.

This may not sound like it has anything to do with healthy eating, but it does. One part of healthy is setting aside some time to eat right. This means you sit down to eat whenever you can, and preferably at a table along with people you love. If you are used to living alone, then this will sound like a pain, but stick with me. Invite some of your friends over to have dinner. Sit around a table and actually talk. You will notice that it helps you to get excited about the food you are cooking and eating. Much like an athletic competition, it will help you to raise your training up to the next level. You can't say the same for eating a pre-fab dinner while sitting in your car or on the couch.

Even if you aren't able to have people over to enjoy dinner with, try to dedicate a space and time for your means, especially dinner and breakfast. These will become very important rituals that you will do for your entire life.

5. Consume more water.

I'm sure you've heard this time and time again that you need to drink eight to ten glasses of water every day. But staying hydrated is very important, especially as a bodybuilder. Hydrated muscles are able to perform and grown at a higher level, and they are protected better against catabolism than when you are dehydrated.

If you can't handle straight water all day long to get in your daily goals, then you can experiment with some other drinks, such as herbal or green tea. You can also flavor your water with lemon, or you can mix in sugar-free electrolytes. You can also have coffee, but if you're serious about being clean, it has to be black and not of that stuff that comes in a fancy cup.

6. Cut back on those added sugars.

Generally speaking, healthy eating doesn't require you to avoid anything in particular. It has more to do with choosing simple and unrefined things. But, if you do want to have an enemy, it should be against added sugars. In their natural state, foods don't contain sugar, except for fruits. Fruits are still good for you. Instead, you need to watch out for all of those sweeteners that have been mixed into things during their manufacturing process.

This can be a hard one to master, but you will have a day when you aren't faced with cravings.

7. Get plenty of fresh produce.

It doesn't matter what type of diet you're following; the golden rule of clean eating is to include as much fresh produce as you can. Vegetables make any diet healthier and better. They will give you nutrients and vitamins to help you feel as good as you look. It will also ensure that you have enough soluble fiber so that you can absorb all of the nutrition that you can get out of the food you eat.

You can't get all of those benefits from a supplement. That supplement will become an excuse you use so that you can cheat when you do get hungry. So make sure that you figure out your favorite fruits and veggies, and you can use the frozen ones if you need to. Also, don't be afraid to use spices and seasonings.

8. Look at your meals as if it's a lifestyle.

Eating clean isn't a diet you have to follow. It is simply a lifestyle that you will be able to sustain from here on out. You don't have to go off the deep end and start throwing out all of the food you love. You can enjoy your food, and you will need to do so in order to stick with this new lifestyle. And you may just have to push yourself so that you start cooking things yourself.

With these eight "rules" in mind, I am fully confident that you will be able to eat clean and enjoy the foods that have.

Chapter 3: Improving Vitality and Energy

Energy and vitality are another issue people have with a plant-based diet. Even those who really want to make the switch are concerned that their energy will plummet, especially for bodybuilders. And I'll be honest, there are some plant-based dieters out there that do suffer from low energy and vitality, but that has more to do with the food they do eat than the food they don't eat. Even plant-based dieters can choose bad foods to eat that harm them more than hurt them. Did you realize Oreos and skittle are vegan? So you see, you can be vegan and eat crap that makes you feel like crap, or, you can be vegan and eat things that make you feel full of time and energetic.

But before we get looking at the foods you are eating to make sure you are gaining energy, we have to look in the obvious places. If you are feeling tired and like your day is dragging, the first thing you need to ask yourself is, "am I getting enough sleep?" Take a look at a five-year-old. Children have more energy than they can use, and they don't get it from energy drinks or coffee. All of that energy comes from the fact that they sleep upwards of ten hours each night. High energy is natural aide effect of a person who is well-rested. So the first thing you need to do is make sure you go to bed by 10 PM, or, depending on when you have to get up, make sure you get at least eight hours.

Secondly, you will want to make sure you are getting plenty of exercise. Of course, this book is geared towards bodybuilders, so that's probably not a problem. But, encase you didn't know, a sedentary life becomes a vicious cycle. When you are sedentary, your heart and muscles lose their ability to handle movement. This causes a lack of energy, which in turn causes you to stay inactive. For a person who has been mainly inactive should start by taking a brisk 30-minute walk each day, and then slowly start to up the intensity so that their heart and joints can keep up.

Thirdly, there can be a medical issue that is causing you to feel a loss of energy. If you were feeling tired before you made the switch to a plant-based diet, you might want to speak with your doctor and get tested for things like depression, thyroid problems, anemia, or other fatigue-causing diseases. Plus, vegan or not, you should probably be on a B12 supplement.

Let's move onto the food. The thing that keeps your muscles revved up is glycogen. If you placed glycogen under a powerful microscope, you would see a long, branching string of beads. All of those beads are molecules of glucose, or, simply put, sugar. Marathoners will often "carbo-load" with rice, pasta, bread, and other starchy foods before their race because as these starches are digested, they will release glucose that body has in the liver and muscles for added energy.

The majority of people would simply be excited that they were able to run a marathon. Brendan Brazier, an endurance athlete, leads the pack in the number of 50k ultramarathons and Ironman triathlons ran, and he believes deeply that food is the number one race fuel for people. He loads his diet full of healthy carbohydrates. When he was first starting his career, he found that animal products would slow his recovery time after exercising. He found that his energy returned quicker when he followed a vegan diet. Then you have Scott Jurek. Jurek ran a 100-mail Western States Endurance Run in 199. He, along with 334 other runners, took off, and Scott didn't just win the race, but he won it every year for six years in a row. He set the course record in 2004 at a time of 15 hours and 36 minutes. Much like Brendan, Scott skips meat lover's pizzas, Western omelet, and all other animal products, and sticks to a carbohydrate loaded vegan menu.

Not All Carbohydrates Are Made The Same

Carbs might be a good source of energy for vegans, but not every carb is created equal. Carbohydrates are meant for staying power. If you look at their glycemic index, you will know which ones are the best. Foods that are placed high on the glycemic index, like white potatoes, wheat, and white bread, sugar, and most cold cereals get digested too quickly and will cause a spike in your blood sugar. Then, once your blood sugar begins to a teaspoon of matcha to six to eight ounces of hot water or steamed milk.

13. Acai Berries

This is a fruit that is native to South and Central America and is high in antioxidants, phytonutrients, minerals, and vitamins. These are things that can help you to fight off disease. Acai berries can help your body when you are exercising and provides you a natural source for sugar. It is a great choice over those sugar sports gels that don't contain important minerals and vitamins.

14. Kale

Everybody knows kale is a big player in the health food department. It is full of dietary fiber, manganese, calcium, vitamin C, and K, and it should be a staple in any bodybuilder's diet. It is considered a superfood and can increase yourathleticism due to its antioxidant levels. The antioxidants in kale can increase your blood oxygen, which will increase your physical stamina.

15. Raisins

This is an easily portable snack that can help to minimize inflammation and provide you with antioxidants. Look at raisins as a healthy carb option that will give you energy for those hard workouts. Add in some to your trail mix if you want.

37

return to your normal, your energy wanes, and you start having cravings.

If you pick foods that are low on the glycemic index, they treat your blood sugar nicer and will help you to avoid those highs and lows. Some of the best choices are sweet potatoes, yams, pasta, pumpernickel or rye bread, beans, and oatmeal. This isn't the only reason to avoid high glycemic foods. There's another reason as well. They will often boost your serotonin levels, which can end up causing you to feel sleepy. This doesn't happen when you choose low glycemic foods. When have that scrambled tofu or veggie bacon in the morning before your bagel, it will help to keep your energy levels from lagging.

Energy Zapping Foods

Besides high glycemic and sugary foods, you also have to watch out for extra fatty foods. You know how you feel have those huge holiday dinners around Thanksgiving, Christmas, or whatever holidays you celebrate? That's caused by all the fat in things like gravy, meats, and cheese. Animal fats and all types of saturated fat can cause your blood to become more viscous, meaning "thicker." You blood basically turns into something like oil instead of staying like water. This is probably the main reason why you end up feeling very tired after those big, heavy meals. This is also a reason why those who go vegan tend to notice their energy levels increase.

Coffee and Energy Drinks

Some people will tell you that both are bad for you and you should cut them out completely. I can't say that because I enjoy a cup of coffee each morning. As for energy drinks, I can say those are bad for you. I use to have one from time to time, but then they started to have adverse effects on me, so I stopped. Plus, they have caused heart problems for many people.

The truth is, wanting that cup of coffee each morning is due to the fact you had coffee the day before are you have to combat the withdrawals. Withdrawals from caffeine are a very real thing and can reduce your mental clarity and alertness, and will create horrible headaches. When you have that morning cup of Joe, it simply hoists you out of those withdrawals, albeit temporarily.

As for energy drinks, like Red Bull, they combine caffeine along with taurine and other additives to improve a person's alertness and athletic performance. Whether their effects are created by the caffeine or everything else in them isn't clear, but people who drink them on a regular basis experience withdrawals from them that are similar to caffeine withdrawal.

In the end, you shouldn't have to rely on caffeine to help with your energy. If you want a cup of coffee, have one. Black coffee isn't going to hurt. But you should have plenty of energy without it, so you should simply enjoy it because you like it and not because you have to have it.

Energy-Boosting Foods

I could make you spend hours looking up the glycemic index of foods, or I could simply give you my top choices for energy and vitality producing vegan-friendly foods. Which would you prefer? We're going to go over some vegan-friendly foods that will help give you energy, and you can choose how you want to enjoy them.

1. Sweet Potatoes

These tubers are a much better alternative to the white potato. They provide loads of minerals and vitamins, such as beta-carotene, manganese, vitamin C, and disease-preventing dietary fiber. These are a great choice for bodybuilders and athletes because when they are consumed in conjunction with protein after your workout, they act as a catalyst to help the protein move into your muscle tissue and start the repairing process.

Sweet potatoes are considered hypoallergenic and are one of the tops sources for post-workout carbs from most exercises, bodybuilders, and athletes who would like to up their energy but keep body fat down. A baked or steamed small to medium sweet potato can be a great post-workout snack.

2. Coconut Oil

This is a good fat full of "medium-chained" fats, which make it very easy to digest, as compared to other dietary fats. They are able to provide an easily accessible source of energy. Coconut oil is also a natural way to increase your metabolism, which gives your body the ability to burn more energy and boosts athletic performance. It also helps the function of the thyroid and gets rid of pancreatic stress, which will make you more active. You can easily add a couple of tablespoons into a smoothie.

3. Bananas

Bananas are a great source of potassium, which is an electrolyte that the body needs but loses when you are exercising. Appalachian State University did a study that found bananas were helpful in fueling cyclist during intense exercise. Bananas are also great at preventing muscle fatigue. Choosing a banana over an energy bar is much better options for some energy. They have a lot less sugar, and they have a lot more nutrients.

4. Rolled Oats

Oats are full of fiber, and they not only reduce your risk of developing heart disease, but they will also slow your glucose absorption, which will help to keep your energy up and your blood sugar levels steady. Oats also have a lot of B vitamins, which helps your body to change carbohydrates into usable energy.

5. Walnuts

Since you won't be getting your Omega-3s from fish, walnuts should be your go-to. They are a great way to get those heart-healthy omega-3 fatty acids. Good fats are a very important part of your diet if you are serious about achieving optimal health and fitness. Healthy fats are able to help heal your body from bruises, sprains, and other tissue injuries, as well as aid in energy production. Unhealthy fats, on the other hand, can slow you down. Have a can of walnuts with your at all times just encase you start feeling sluggish, or, if you make your own trail mix, add in some walnuts.

6. Lentils

Lentils are full of dietary fiber, containing eight grams in a half-cup serving. They are also great at keeping you feeling fuller for longer, and they will keep your energy levels up for your busy day.

7. Coconut Water

If you are getting tired of drinking plain water, then you should try out some coconut water. There is only a mild coconut flavor, but it is full of important electrolytes. A lot of the sports drink on the market that have a lot of added sugars that play a part in diabetes and weight gain. Coconut water, on the other hand is a natural way to consume electrolytes with no additional sugars. You don't have to consume as much coconut water to get the beneficial minerals you need, so you won't end up feeling bloated or full like you would with other electrolyte drinks.

8. Spinach

Spinach is full of folic acid and B vitamins, and both of these will provide you with lots of energy. Spinach can easily be added into different meals, from smoothies to scrambles and casseroles.

9. Oranges

If you need a quick boost of energy, oranges should be your go-to food. It is full of natural sugars, and they will also give you three grams of fiber, which can help to sustain your energy levels. A single navel orange will help you to meet your daily requirement for vitamin C.

10. Avocados

This delicious fruit is a great source of healthy fats that can activate your body. Your body can also utilize it for fuel to help you through your day or workout. It is also a great source of B6, folic acid, vitamin K, fiber, and vitamin C. Vitamin C is a great antioxidant that will help to support your adrenal glands, which you can end up overworking during stressful times. While B vitamins help with several functions within the body, they are often seen as the "stress and energy" vitamins. During a workout, your body becomes very stressed, so avocados work like a magic fruit.

11. Olive Oil

Olive oil is praised all of the time for its health-promoting properties. It can help increase your healthy cholesterol levels, protect your blood vessels, and fight off free-radical damage. Most athletes who push themselves to the limit each and every day have to consume large amounts of calories to keep up with all of the energy they use, so try to add in a couple of tablespoons of EVOO to food that you have already cooked can help add some nutrient-dense calories and healthy fats.

12. Matcha

This is a powdered form of green tea, but matcha tends to be better for you than regular green tea. It has five times the amount of l-theanine, which is an amino acid that promotes a focused and relaxed mental state. While matcha does have caffeine, like every other green tea, it contains enough l-theanine to get rid of the jitters that caffeine can cause for some people. That means you get high energy and intense focus without all of those ticks. Coffee does have some health benefits, but green tea also contains a lot of antioxidants that will help you to protect yourself from oxidative stress and fend off disease. Add a half of

16. Apricots

The last food on this list is apricots. There are some people who believe if they don't eat before a workout, they will end up burning more fat. While this may be true in some instances, it can also cause people to become dizzy, nausea, and lack important energy, which will hinder your ability to get the workout you want. Having a simple snack of an apricot before you workout can help give you the nutrients you need as well as an easily digested fuel to prevent all of those nasty side effects.

If you make sure you consume these energy-producing foods, along with others, you will never be lacking in energy or vitality. And, since you were a bodybuilder first, you should easily be able to slide into a plant-based diet that is full of these healthy energy-inducing foods without having to think about it.

Chapter 4:Picking The Right Foods

Learning what foods you should choose, and how to make sure you get plenty of protein and calories, is what will help you jump on the plant-based bandwagon with easy. Before we start discussing foods and numbers, I want to divert for a second to a semi-related topic. I have used the terms plant-based and vegan interchangeably throughout this book, but I wanted to make sure you understand that it is possible for a person to be on a plant-based diet and not be vegan. If a person tells you they follow a plant-based diet, you can't be certain they eat vegan or not because plant-based diet could simply mean they incorporate more plant products and proteins into their diet, but they still consume some animal products.

I wanted to be clear, from this point on, the plant-based I am talking about is a completely vegan diet. I'm sure you already figured that out, but I want to let you know that just because somebody says plant-based doesn't necessarily mean vegan. This could save you at dinner parties in the future.

Now we can move into building a vegan diet for a bodybuilder. I'm certain you already know this, but there are many different categories of bodybuilding. You have the traditional bodybuilding, and you also have physique, figure, and bikini. As a whole, no matter the type, bodybuilding will require a person to lose fat as well as put on muscle. Bodybuilders are able to do this through a combination of diet and strength training, and, by the time competition day rolls around, they are posing across the stage with a low body fat ratio.

But let's be real, building muscle is hard work no matter the diet you follow. And, if you are brand new to a plant-based lifestyle, supporting your athletic work with a vegan diet can be tough as well.

But it is possible, and easy, to slim down and bulk up while following a plant-based diet. It will require some nutrition strategies and proactive meal planning, just like competitive bodybuilding and smart vegan eating.

Bodybuilding Nutrition

If you are serious about being a vegan bodybuilding, you are going to have to have a good understanding of basic bodybuilding 'rules' for nutrition and food. The majority of bodybuilders, no matter what they eat, will split their season into two separate phases: bulking and cutting. With the bulking phase, they will consume a protein-rich and high-calorie diet, and they will strength train intensely to add as much muscle as they can. Then they will start the cutting phase. This is where they work to decrease their body fat, which usually done by slowly cutting down the fat and calorie intake.

These phases, both, will require the correct amount of calories and the best balance of fats, proteins, and carbs. This is the trifecta of nutrients that will help you to drop weight, become stronger, and recover.

The actual breakdown of macronutrients for each person is going to be slightly different. The majority of bodybuilders will have a coach or nutritionist that they work with to help them figure out their macro and calorie needs in each phase. But, there are some macro and calorie basics that you may find helpful, but we'll talk about that in a minute.

Calorie Intake

While calorie counting is a touchy subject among many, some will argue that it is better that you don't do it, for bodybuilders, it plays a big part in their nutrition. When your goals are to add muscle mass, you have to make sure that your body has the fuel it needs to increase and build the size of the muscle fibers. And if you start reducing your calorie intake, you will start losing fat. This helps to make you look more muscular, even though you aren't gaining new muscle.

You have to know what your true calorie needs are. You can't guess, estimate, or assume things about your habits. You need to use real data that is based upon what you do and who you are.

Since not everybody is the same, you can't give a baseline number for how many calories you need to consume. But lucky for you, there are a lot of online calculators that can do the math for you. Head over to bodybuilding.com and use their online calculator to figure out how many calories you should be aiming for during your different phases.

The numbers you get from these calculators should only be used as a starting point, and then you can start to experiment with those numbers to figure out what works best for you. The reason you have to play around with it is due to things like sleep quality, stress levels, hydration, metabolism, activity level, and menstrual cycle. They all affect the number of calories you need, just like muscle gain, loss, and maintenance.

This goes for vegan and omnivorous bodybuilders alike. Your daily calorie intake isn't going to differ, no matter what diet you follow. Some like to think that vegans have to eat more calories, but that's simply not true.

Now, I know I just dangled an online calorie counter in front of your face, and you are free to use it, but you can also figure out some numbers on your own. Don't worry, though, it isn't nearly as complicated as it may sound. You first have to start with figuring out your BMR, which is your basal metabolic rate with the Harris-Benedict equation. BMR is how many calories you expend through simply existing. This is based upon your weight, height, age, and gender. You can get your BMR using the calculator at globalrph.com.

Now you will take that number and combine it with your actual activity level. This is an additional movement other than just existing. This would include things like walking upstairs, going to the gym, running errands, or walking the dog. This will provide you with the approximate number of calories that you expend each day, which is considered your calorie needs. The calculator at globalrph.com takes this into consideration.

That means if you expend 2500 calories each day, you will have to eat 2500 calories to make sure that you maintain that weight. If you wanted to gain muscle, you are going to have to eat more than 2500 calories, which should come mostly from real plant foods. Mix that with some resistance weight training, and then you will be well on your way to more muscle.

While this may sound simple, implementing this into your life can be a struggle. But, trust me, it doesn't have to be that way. You simply need to focus on consuming healthy foods that you love along with enough calories, and you shouldn't have a problem. To figure out the right foods for you, you also have to think about the nutrient density of them.

Nutrient Density

Nutrient density of food refers to how many nutrients you will get from it, given how many calories it has. Nutrients are what provide your body with nourishment, energy, muscle recovery, allows for growth, and maintains life. Think about phytonutrients, nitric oxide, water, fiber, antioxidants, amino acids, minerals, and vitamins. If you want to go for foods with lots of nutrients, then you will want to aim for whole foods.

If you think about it, whole foods don't contain anything that shouldn't be there. There is a big difference between eating 2500 calories of plant foods like seeds, nuts, grains, veggies, and fruits and eating 2500 calories of ice cream, candy, pizza, and friends. You're getting 2500 calories both ways, but only one of them will provide you with all of the necessary nutrients that you need.

That means low-calorie, nutrient-dense foods are going to give you bigger rewards than foods that are high in calories, cut contain few nutrients. If you eat a high-calorie, nutrient-poor diet, you are going to struggle to reach your fitness goals, no matter what those goals may be.

Dr. Joel Fuhrman came up with the ANDI score that helps you to know the nutrient density of foods. ANDI means Aggregate Nutrient Density Index. It shows you the "nutrients divided by calories," of different foods. The higher a food scores on the ANDI scale, the more nutrients it contains.

If you shop at Whole Foods, especially if you get the salad bar, you have probably noticed that signs that show the ANDI score of some of the foods. While it may seem weird to boil all of the nutritional information for foods down to one number, I think it's helpful. And this score doesn't mean that you can only eat the highest scoring foods and ignore the others, but when you are trying to eat a varied and healthy diet, it gives you a way to rank your foods and make sure you are making good choices.

The scores for the ANDI scale ranges from 1 to 1000. 1000 is the most nutrient-dense food, whereas 1 is the least nutrient-dense. There are a lot of interesting results, but most of them aren't that surprising. As you would guess, leafy greens top the charts and are following by other vegetables, fruits, seeds and nuts, beans, animal products, and then junk foods. Here's a list of foods that will help give you an idea of what the ANDI score of you favorite foods look like:

- Kale, Collard Greens, Mustard Greens, and Watercress – 1000

- Swiss Chard – 895

- Bok Choy – 865

- Spinach – 707

- Arugula – 604

- Romaine – 510

- Brussels Sprouts – 490

- Carrots – 458

- Cabbage – 434

- Broccoli – 340

- Cauliflower – 315

- Bell Peppers – 265

- Asparagus – 205

- Strawberries – 182

- Sweet Potato – 181

- Artichoke – 145

- Blueberries – 132

- Grapes and Pomegranates – 119

- Cantaloupe – 118

- Onions – 109

- Orange – 98

- Peaches – 65

- Cherries – 55

- Pineapple – 54

- Apple and Mango – 53

- Shrimp – 36

- Salmon – 34

- Eggs and 1% Milk – 31

- Chicken Breast – 24

- Lean Ground Beef – 21

- Feta Cheese – 20

- French Fries – 12

- Cheddar Cheese, White Pasta, and Apple Juice – 11

- Vanilla Ice Cream – 9

- Cola – 1

While counting calories is important when it comes to weight loss and gain, nutrient density looks at a person's overall health and nutrition. Plant foods will provide you the right combination of low-calorie and high-nutrient foods that you need to be healthy.

As you should know by now, being vegan doesn't mean you have to limit yourself to fewer foods than an omnivore eats. You have a lot of options at your disposal, but this can also end up becoming overwhelming for some.

Macro Breakdown

A big mistake that people will make when they start following a vegan bodybuilding diet is that they forget to eat enough good calories, which can end up hurting the muscle-building goals. To make sure you are getting quality calories, you will need to know its macro breakdown.

Macronutrients, as mentioned before, are fat, carbohydrates, and protein. They are all major nutrients that your body has to have in order to function efficiently and properly. Counting your macros simply ensures that you consume a certain balance of each macro every day. Following a macro diet is also considered a flexible diet because you are allowed to consume whatever you want as long as you hit your numbers.

And guess what? This breakdown is the same for vegans and meat-eaters alike. The amount of macronutrients you need to consume is going to remain the same. The only difference is you will use vegan foods to reach it. There aren't any hard-and-fast rules as to what your macro breakdown needs to be, and your ratios will probably change depending on where competition day is sitting. For bodybuilders, you typically want to keep your carbs up, fats moderate, and protein high enough to help support the growth of muscle. Then you will typically cut that right before a competition by decreasing your carb intake a lot and your fat intake slightly.

For example, a general guideline breakdown ratio is 20/60/20 of fat, carb, and protein. This doesn't mean you have to follow those numbers exactly. You can play around with it and figure out which ratio works for you. Chances are if you have been a bodybuilder for awhile, you already have a breakdown you have been following, and you can continue to follow that ratio.

Vegan Protein

We've already discussed how a vegan diet is not low in protein, and that a vegan can consume just as much protein as a meat-eater. But it's also understandable that bodybuilders are worried that they won't be able to reach their protein needs since they do tend to eat more protein than the average person.

There are a lot of different vegan protein sources out there, more than people know. You have hemp seeds, vital wheat gluten, fava beans, seitan, tempeh, bean pasta, textured vegetable protein, tofu, and lupini beans, just to name a few.

There is also vegan protein powder that you can use in place of whey protein in smoothies, and research has found that it is just as effective as whey protein. Oatmeal, black beans, kidney beans, nuts, nut butters, and amaranth are other great protein options for vegans. And there are even some foods that you wouldn't think contains protein that does, such as Brussels sprouts, mushrooms, chlorella, greens, and potatoes.

But it's also important to note that never single vegan protein option is created equal. Proteins contain amino acids. There are some amino acids, however, that are seen as "nonessential." This means that your body is able to make that particular amino acid on its own. There are some amino acids, though, that are "essential." This means that your body is unable to make it on its own without food.

There are nine essential amino acids that your body has to have in order to perform different functions, such as building muscles. Every animal protein source, such as fish, beef, eggs, dairy, pork, chicken, and turkey, contains all of these. When it comes to plant-based protein sources, they don't all contain all nine of these. But there are three exceptions: soy, buckwheat, and quinoa. Those three do contain all nine essential amino acids.

However, if you make a point of eating a variety of plant foods, your body will be able to store all of those amino acids and then combine them to create a complete protein. For example, beans and rice on their own aren't complete proteins, but when you eat them both, they will provide you with all of the essential amino acids you need.

Mix in an Effective Exercise Program

We've covered a lot on the nutrition portion of this chapter, but before you get the thought that you can gain muscle through food alone, you also have to have an effective exercise program. I'm here to talk about food, so I won't get into this a lot, and hopefully, you already have an exercise routine. But I would like to share some fundamental pieces of information you should follow.

1. The foundation for your workout should be dumbbell and barbell exercises.

2. Do exercises that you like to do. Ultimately, if you aren't having fun, then you are going to try to find a way to avoid doing it.

3. Have a workout plan that will target all of your major muscle groups, which includes abs, arms, shoulders, back, chest, and legs, to make sure that you stimulate growth in every around of your body and not just your biceps and chest. You can either choose to focus on one muscle group during your workouts, or you can mix up workouts to target it all of them.

4. The most important part is consistency. You have to put in enough time in order to get the results you want.

5. Create goals that you can reach.

6. Document all of your workouts so that you can hold yourself accountable. You want to train consistently and keep a level of intensity that is going to elicit and ignite change.

It is important that you track your workouts along with your food. While this may seem like a waste of time, or super tedious, it will be worth it in the long run. Things will become second nature. And you may find that meal tracking is the secret to reaching all of your bodybuilding goals. You have the tools you need, so now you just have to do it.

have to watch out for the refined sugars and other sweets so that your bad bacteria stay in check.

Do You Have a Bad Gut?

There was a time when the digestive system was viewed as a "simple" body system made up of one long tube that all of our food moved through, was absorbed, and then excreted. Food isn't the only thing that can through your gut health out of whack. High stress, not enough sleep, and of course bad foods and antibiotics can damage your microbiome. This can end up affecting several different aspects of your health, including your hormones, weight, skin, immune system, heart, and brain. There are several different signs of an unhealthy gut that you can be on the lookout for.

1. Upset Stomach

Stomach issues like heartburn, diarrhea, constipation, bloating, and gas are all signs of an unhappy gut. When you have a balanced gut, you will have a lot less difficulty in processing your foods and eliminating waste.

2. Sugary Diet

If you are eating a lot of processed foods with added sugars, you are hurting the good bacteria in your gut. The imbalance this causes will lead to more sugar cravings, which will only continue to hurt your gut. Consuming high amounts of refined sugars

57

have been links to more inflammation. Inflammation plays a big role in several diseases and cancer.

3. Unintentional Weight Loss or Gain

If you lose or gain weight without making extensive changes to your exercise or diet habit, it could be signaling an unhealthy gut. A gut that is imbalanced can end up impairing your body's ability to store fat, regulate blood sugar, and absorb nutrients. You could lose weight because of small intestinal bacterial overgrowth, but you could end up gaining weight because of insulin resistance, or it urges you to overeat because of decreased nutrient absorption.

4. Fatigue and Sleep Disturbances

Having an unhealthy gut can cause sleep disturbances like poor sleep or insomnia, which can cause chronic fatigue. Most of your body's serotonin, which affects sleep and a mood, is produced in your gut. When your gut is hurt, it can impair your ability to sleep. There are some sleep problems that have been connected to a greater risk of developing fibromyalgia.

5. Skin Irritation

Problems with the skin, like eczema, have been related to gut damage. Inflammation within the gut created by food allergies or a poor diet can create the "leaking" of proteins out into areas of the body that they shouldn't be, which can end up irritating skin and causing different problems.

6.   Autoimmune Conditions

Medical research has found that a bad gut can cause a lot of problems for the immune system. It is believed that an unhealthy gut could increase systemic inflammation and affect the proper functioning of your immune system. This will end up leading to autoimmune disorders, where the body starts to attack itself and not harmful invaders.

7.   Food Intolerances

Food intolerances are caused by your body having problems digesting certain types of food. This is very different than a food allergy, which is due to an immune response to certain foods. It is believed that food intolerances could be due to poor quality of bacteria in the digestive system. This can end up causing difficulty in digesting certain foods and other unpleasant symptoms, like nausea, abdominal pain, diarrhea, gas, and bloating.

Testing Your Bowel

There is a bit of a "fun" test you can do to see how well your digestive system is actually functioning. This is essentially a bowel transit time test. You will need some charcoal tablets to do this.

You will begin by taking five grams of the charcoal and make a note of the exact date and time you took them. This is very important. If you don't note the time, you won't be able to figure out an accurate reading. Then, you wait. When you have to use the bathroom, you will start looking for dark stools. Once you do notice your stool has become darkened by the charcoal, note the time. See how many hours have passed since you took the charcoal and when your stool became darker. That's your bowel transit time.

If the time was less than 12 hours, then you have likely not been absorbing all of the nutrients you need to.

If it is between 12 and 24 hours, then your body is absorbing the nutrients that it needs. This is a transit time that you want to have.

If it takes more than 24 hours, food is being held in your color for too long. This could cause a problem because substances that need to be eliminated are getting a chance to move back into your blood, and it is upping your risk of colon disease.

Your Digestive System

Let's take a moment to talk about your digestive system. Picture your digestive system as a 25 to 35-foot long hose that travels from your mouth to your anus. The lining of this replaces itself every three to five days.

The basic functioning of the digestive system is to break down food into little bits that the cells of your body are able to use for growth, repair, energy, and more. As food moves through this system, it gets broken down into glycerol, glucose, and amino acids, depending on what types of food you are eating.

The hardest part about this, for most, is that you can be eating what most would think is a healthy diet, but they can still be faced with issues. Basically, it won't matter what you are eating if you aren't able to absorb those foods correctly because of a digestive disorder.

Digestion actually starts in the brain. Do you remember learning about Pavlov's Dog, the most famous example of classical conditioning? Basically, Ivan Pavlov rang a bell each time he fed his dog. Eventually, his dog would start to salivate simply from the sound of the ringing bell. Basically, the dog's body was getting ready for the digestion process, and this also occurs for humans.

Once you place food in your mouth, salivary amylase will continue this process through the act of breaking carbs into maltose. This is done by breaking the bonds that hold carbohydrate molecules together and produces tri- and disaccharides.

Once you swallow, the food moves through your esophagus. This tube moves the food from the mouth all the way into the stomach, and this little ride for the food only takes around five to six seconds. But it can take as long as a minute if you did not chew your food very well.

Lastly, you have a flap connected to the bottom of your esophagus that is known as the esophageal sphincter. This sphincter, in an ideal world, is supposed to stay closed, so that food and acid remains in your stomach and doesn't travel back up into your esophagus. If it doesn't, this is what causes acid reflux, or it can even cause a hiatal hernia.

Once the food reaches the stomach, it will liquefy the food into a gooey liquid known as chyme. Then HCL will start to break apart all of the protein chains into little pieces. Chyme and HCL are super acidic. In fact, if HCL touched your skin, it would cause a bad burn. HCL also sterilizes food by killing off bad microbes that could still be on the food.

Your stomach has a protective layer of mucus that contains the HCL so that it doesn't burn through everything, but you have probably heard of people who have had an ulcer. An ulcer is created when this protective layer breaks down; the HCL in the stomach burns a hold in the stomach. Ulcers can be healed, though, before they require surgery.

The stomach also produces pepsin, which helps break proteins down. There is also lipase, which breaks down fat. While most of the nutrients get absorbed later on in its journey, ethyl alcohol, some salt, and water heads right into your blood. This is why you feel the effects of alcohol quickly. Food remains in the stomach for about two to four hours, depending on what you ate because fat and fiber will slow down this process.

Then things move onto the small intestine. This area is about 15 to 20 feet long. This is the main place where food is digested. The fingerlike folds, called villi, absorb all of the nutrients from your food. The villi and microvilli are what make you the intestinal wall and produce digestive enzymes and blocks out possible harmful substances.

There are actually some medications and foods that can cause the intestinal wall to end up losing its ability to figure out the things it should absorb and which it shouldn't, which is what causes leaky gut syndrome.

Continue on your food's journey; it will hit the duodenum first. This is where magnesium, manganese, copper, calcium, and other minerals are absorbed. Digesting fat and water-soluble vitamins start here, so does the fat digestion and other types of carbs. If your HCL levels were too low, these nutrients wouldn't be able to be absorbed.

Then it hits the jejunum, which takes up 40% of the rest of your intestines. There are intestinal brushes here that secrete different enzymes that help your body absorb other types of carbs. There are some water-soluble B vitamins that start their digestion here, along with amino acids and protein.

Then it hits the last and largest part of the intestines called the ileum. This is the part of your intestines that absorb bile salts, B12, and cholesterol. Then it hits the large intestine, and this is what is responsible for absorbing water and any other nutrients that remain. This is a big part of staying hydrated.

That's it for how food gets digested, but now you should be able to see how important your digestive system is, and we didn't even talk about what the other organs do as well.

When your gut health is off, it throws this whole process out of whack, but there are things you can do to fix this problem.

Improving Gut Health

There are a lot of different things you can do to improve gut health. Let's take a look at some things you can start going.

1. Take a Probiotic or Prebiotics

Replenishing your bacterial flora is one way you can help your gut. When buying probiotics, the best ones will likely need to be refrigerated, and you should aim for ones that contain lactobacillus acidophilus and bifidobacteria bifidum.

You can also take prebiotics, which basically fuels your bacteria, whereas probiotics are the actual bacteria. Prebiotics are nutrients that are non-digestible, and your good bacteria are able to use them for energy. They help to stimulate the growth of your good bacteria. There are some prebiotic foods like chicory, leeks, onion, garlic, bananas, and artichokes.

2.   Eat Flora Enhancing Food

These foods are always fermented. A lot of people will turn to cultured dairy products like yogurt and kefir, but as a vegan, you can't have those. Don't worry, though, sauerkraut and kimchi can become your two new best friends. They are delicious, and your gut will thank you for them.

3.   Fibrous Carbs

When picking your carbs, go with carbs that are more fibrous because it takes longer for them to be digested. You don't want to go crazy with the fiber right off the bat because you can shock your body. Slowly start to add more fiber into your diet, and don't worry about soluble versus insoluble. You want to focus on your total grams.

4. Get Rid of The Garbage

If you haven't already, you need to lower your intake of alcohol, trans fats, and refined carbs.

5. Reduce Stress

Stress can mess your gut as well, so do your best to lower your stress levels to help your gut out. Try adding some meditation into your workout routines, or even some yoga.

Chapter 6:Bodybuilding Advice Mistakes

Being an athlete is hard. You have limited time, and it is hard to manage your training with your normal everyday life. Everybody is throwing different ideas and tips your way whether or not they are qualified to do so. It is hard to know what tips to follow and which ones to totally ignore.

Do you love going to the gym? Before you pack that bag, look at some advice from other athletes to make sure you are making some of these common mistakes. You've probably seen some crazy stuff while at the gym. That guy using that piece of equipment wrong. Someone using the chest machine to blast their lower body. Rowers get used to strengthen hamstrings. How about those people trying to use the pull-down machine and end up turning themselves into a yo-yo? If you haven't had the pleasure of seeing it for yourself, you might have seen some fails on videos.

Even though they are embarrassing and some are cringe-worthy, what is more dangerous than all of these blunders are the small mistakes that put you are risk for an injury or will hamper your goals.

You will make mistakes; there's no doubt about it. The thing that matters is the amount of time you take to figure out these mistakes and correct them. Mistakes are going to happen at the gym, and some are even encouraged. How will you figure out your personal best on squats or your maximum box-jump height if you stop before you fail smart? Staying away from unnecessary mistakes is the key to preventing harm to your body and sparing with your ego. Here are some of the biggest mistakes that people make at the gym. Pay attention to what you read here and make sure you don't commit any of these:

- Making the Motions

Many people at the gym are just "going through the motions." Don't leave your brain outside and become a victim of redundancy. Everyone likes having a routine, but if you do the same program over and over again and never challenge yourself, you are going to plateau.

If you get bored with your routine and have checked out mentally, your progress is going to taper off until you just don't do it anymore.

- No Goals

You've probably heard the old saying: "If you fail to plan, you plan to fail." I have seen numerous bodybuilders walk into the gym and ask their trainer:

"What should we do today?"

"You want to work on your biceps and chest?"

"Sure, that sounds fine."

If you don't set any goals, you will not have a sense of direction with your training, and you won't try to find the progress you want because of this.

You can correct this by setting some goals and working toward them. Anybody who is successful will plan and set goals and will have a goal for every aspect of their lives. This holds true for the top businessmen all the way to the top athletes. All these people have one thing in common. They all set goals. Setting goals is relatively simple and easy to do, but the benefits they give you are invaluable. Goals make you focus your attention and will clarify what you want to achieve.

Here are a few tips to help you set goals:

1. Create short-term goals: These are your stepping stones to help you reach your long term goal. If your long term goal s to squat 350 pounds by the end of next year, then set a short-term goal of how much weight you need to squat each month to reach this long-term goal. It is easier to reach one goal either daily or weekly, like increasing 2.5 to 5 pounds each week, than to think you have to increase your bench presses by 50 pounds a week.

2. Stay realistic: Make sure your goals are achievable. If your expectations are way too high, you will lose confidence and get frustrated with yourself. Be sure that your goals aren't too easy for you. They need to be challenging enough that you have to work to reach them.

3. Measurable goals: If you set a goal of "I want to be fit," it doesn't give you anything specific to strive for. You have to be decisive in the things you want to achieve and how soon you want to achieve it. You need to set something like: "I want to be able to run a 5k in less than 20 minutes by December 2020.

- Not Getting Enough Downtime

People don't give their central nervous system time to recover. You need to divide up your training, so you don't get discouraged if you don't see any progress.

After you have finished eight weeks of intense training, take a week off to recover. This is the best thing you can do to make sure you keep coming back stronger than ever.

- Not Warming Up

I have been in many gyms and watched people just go right over to the leg press machine or bench press rack and began doing set without doing any warm-up at all. Trainers shouldn't allow this at all. If the person doesn't have a trainer, the gym should have people that watch out for ones who don't know exactly what they are doing.

Warming up is very important before you do any workout. It doesn't matter if you are getting ready to lift weights or run a 5k. The question you might have is, why is this so important?

The simple answer is that it gets the joints and muscles ready for a larger level of activity. It has some benefits, too:

1. Neuromuscular coordination gets improved when you warm up before you do any type of movement

2. Increases how efficient oxygen is used in the muscles that have been warmed up

3. It can increase the blood circulation to the muscles

4. Gets rid of lactic acid that gets accumulated during earlier workouts

5. It increases how fast the muscles relax and contract

6. It reduces muscle stiffness

Warming up is easy to do. It just takes five minutes of stretching, or jogging and some certain drills.

- Doing the Same Workout Over and Over Again

Repetition is another huge mistake. Progressive overload can't be emphasized enough when beginning a fitness program. Most people will do the same three sets of 10 to 12 reps using the same weights every day for numerous months.

When you are just beginning, three sets of ten reps are going to give you results. But you are going to need to add more weight or more reps to continue to progress.

- Ignoring Your Weaknesses

You've heard the old saying: "A chain is only as strong as its weakest link." How many times have you seen athletes ignore the entire part of their training all because they know it is their weakness? Because of their ego, they don't feel like they have to show anyone.

The bad news for these people is their weaknesses are normally highlighted by their constant refusal. If you truly want to be the best you can be, you have to begin working on your weaknesses and change them into your strengths.

When you work on your weaknesses, it can be hard, especially if you have a large ego. You need to remind yourself about the old saying above. You will get better if you will work on fixing your weaknesses.

There are five steps you need to do when designing a routine to work on your weakness:

1. Create a goal

2. Do some tests to figure out your current fitness level.
    These tests need to look at your body composition,
    maximum sprint, agility, anaerobic endurance, aerobic
    endurance, anaerobic power, and maximum strength.

3. Do a gap analysis. Find the areas that need improvement.

4. Figure out a training program that will work on
    maintaining your strength and improving your
    weaknesses.

5. Each month you need to monitor your progress and make
    adjustments when needed.

- Going with the Flow

Following what everyone else is doing only applies to people
who want to take the stage and make fitness their career. Most
new fitness models won't do anything to separate them from the
rest of the models. You have to do something to make yourself
stand out above the crowd. Do something that will draw people
to you. If you are just like everybody else, your career is going to
be extremely short.

- Not Enough Recovery Time

Many training partners like pushing their people too far, and
this is the foundation of creating a bad training routine.

Letting your muscles repair and rebuild all the small tears that get created because of training, is the key to increasing your muscle size and strength. When you train during times where you are in pain, you are only slowing down your opportunity to make progress on building your muscles.

You need to take the time to have enough recovery time between your workouts. The key to creating a sufficient recovery for your muscles is to listen to your body. If your muscles are very sore before a workout, then you have been overtraining.

Your workout routine needs to be constructed so that you can recover totally before your next workout. You don't need to make sprints the day after you have done a lot of lower bodyweight training.

You need to remain consistent with your nutrition (this gets covered later) to make sure that you are getting the right amount of protein because this plays a huge role in repairing your muscles.

If you constantly have problems with your recovery, then some techniques like post-workout stretches, ice massages, and contrast showers can help you out.

- Choosing the Wrong Program

Figuring out the right exercise program for you is necessary. Instead of putting together a program quickly and hopping from one machine to the next, you should go to the gym with a plan in mind. Your exercise routine needs to reflect your goal. It doesn't matter whether you just want to gain strength, get leaner, or bulking up.

People normally follow a routine that doesn't have any direction or doesn't target a certain muscle group. At times, they will tweak their routine rather than following instructions.

You may think that you are advanced enough to make some changes to a program by yourself, but this isn't usually the case. Just one alteration will change your whole result.

- Not Getting Any Stronger

Even though getting stronger isn't the main reason for creating larger muscles, it is a big part for some bodybuilders, especially people just starting out and intermediate.

Your largest muscles aren't your strongest ones. Your strongest muscles aren't your largest. If you don't build up to lifting a decent amount of weight for the right amount of reps in the right technique, you aren't going to develop decent muscles.

- Bad Form

Improper form is another mistake that many people make. Some people will use too much weight and can't even complete one full set. They will rock in order to get the weights up, and his is doing them any good at all. Bad form will target the wrong muscles and will reinforce poor patterns within your movements. If you are sure the right way to do an exercise, ask somebody who will know. Never be afraid to approach a trainer if you feel like you aren't doing something just right. You might just keep yourself away from an injury.

You should never increase the amount of weight you are trying to lift until you can do an exercise the right way in a full range of motion. When you have found the correct form and muscle isolation, you can then add more weights. It is better to use good form and lift lighter weights than push yourself and get sloppy.

- Using Weights Wrong

Getting stronger is important; poundage is a progress killer. There are bodybuilders who can't manage weights correctly.

Try cutting back your weights by ten percent, work on your technique until it is perfect, and then in the next month or so, build the amount of weight back up while keeping the perfect form. You should soon see some new growth. Next, work on adding more pounds to gain more growth.

- No Training

Just going to the gym can be a huge hurdle for some people. The biggest mistake is not doing any training at all. Yes, the gym can be intimidating, especially if you are just starting out. If you can head in with a program in mind that will fit your goals, you can seek support from other people at the gym. This can give you a boost to your confidence that will take the guesswork out of the picture.

- Adding Weights Too Fast

Adding five or ten pounds at a time isn't a good way to go. If you aren't a beginner, you build strength slowly.

After you are at your best weight, add a little iron to your next workout. Use just a one-pound bar and then in a week or so add another. Most gyms won't have the smallest weights, so you will need to get your own and take them with you.

- Using Weights and Overdoing the Cardio

The worst mistake I've seen at the gym is people using the cardio equipment trying to lose weight. If you want to lose pounds, many people first choice is to jump on the treadmill, elliptical, or bike to try to "feel the burn" and sweat off the calories. Yes, cardio can help you get rid of energy, but lifting weights is what will reshape your body. This is what will give you your desired results.

Most women are afraid to lift weights because they don't want to look manly. Just remember that women don't possess the right levels of testosterone to create a lot of bulk. Just building a decent amount of muscle can take calories, energy, and time.

This makes it a dedication-driven and slow process. Thinking that you are going to wake up the next day looking like Arnold Schwarzenegger is completely off base.

- Doing Whatever You Can to Avoid Injuries

An injury will kill your progress. Using the right exercise techniques is necessary for your training safely. You can't blast into a rep. You can't have an excessive range of motion. You can't heave, drop, yank, or have anybody English. Don't just give the old cliché: "Use good technique" lip service.

Figuratively tattoo it into your forehead and take heed. Changing up your technique in the middle of training can be a devastating mistake. Being disciplined in your training is all about good technique and effort. Training safely involves changing your exercise program up to make it individual to you.

If you are doing an exercise and it begins to hurt, but you know that you have been doing the right technique along with the right rep speed, you have done some good modifications; you might need to drop that exercise. The main rule to exercising is: "Do no harm." You have to get rid of "No pain, no gain."

- No Training Partner

Having a training partner can boost your intensity and zeal. Find someone who has the same ability to recover as you, so you can use the same or similar training program. Then you can push each other to do the perfect workout each time. Just make sure you use a disciplined, correct, progressive, and intensive technique.

Having a partner who isn't right for you could cause your complete undoing. If they can recover faster than you can, tolerate more exercises and reps. If they push you to abuse intensity enhancers and forced reps, you need to get rid of them completely.

- Doing Too Many Sets

Don't do any more than three sets for each exercise and then a maximum of eight exercises for every routine. If you can handle more than three sets for each exercise, you aren't doing enough. You need to train harder, so you don't want to ever do more than three sets for each exercise.

- Weight Train

You need to do weight training at least three days every week. You can divide your entire program into three parts, such as:

1. Triceps, delts, and chest

2. Neck, biceps, and back

3. Calves, thighs, and abs

Make sure you hit every body part at least once a week or split it into two parts, such as:

1. Neck, triceps, delts, and chest

2. Biceps, back, calves, thighs, and abs

Then you can alternate these two workouts so that you hit every area three times in two weeks. You could also try one option for a few months, then change to another one for another couple of months and see which will work out best for you.

- Not Enough Effort

If you are just walking around at the gym without doing anything, you aren't going to produce growth. You don't ever have to train until you drop, you do need to train hard. Do you actually do every rep you possibly can in every set without compromising your technique? If you don't, begin now and put more effort into it.

- No Deadlifting

You need to learn how to deadlift. This is the most productive exercise to help you build mass. You need to master how to do the deadlift right. You can do a partial life from your knees or do a conventional style. In a few years, you will have built up your muscles into something very impressive.

Perfect technique is necessary. You have to stay away from any exaggerated range of motion. You have to deadlift safely and right or don't do it at all.

- No Squats

You have to learn how to do squats right and intensively. Squats are just beneficial to just the lower back, glutes, and thighs. It can have an effect on your entire body. There are some people who can't squat intensively and safely, many can.

Love the squat, improve on your technique, and you will help your gains. Be sure you are squatting the right way and doing it safely. If you can't, don't do it.

- Being Focused on Wrong Exercises

Give the building exercises more priority than the detail ones. Even though certain exercises do have valuable roles, the major builders of muscles are the large compound exercises like:

1. Chins

2. Rows

3. Dips

4. Bench presses

5. Deadlifts

6. Leg presses

7. Squats

You need to get good at these and use a decent weight if you want to build your muscles.

Things That Are Messing Up Your Gains

Don't allow your muscles to go away after your breakthrough. There are some intermediate level mistakes that can leave you frustrated while the other people at the gym keep getting bigger.

All the internet hype about fitness has gotten a bad rap. Yes, there are plenty of advice and lots of hate, but more people are getting educated about the principles of muscle growth.

First of all, they lift. This is a huge step, especially for women. Second, they understand the critical role that recovery and nutrition play. They also recognize that the main factor to progressing is just following a program faithfully and consistently for several months.

Will this be enough? For a little bit, it will. But all of a sudden, you aren't going to be a beginner anymore. You have turned into an intermediate lifter. This sounds wonderful, but this only means that you have to work harder to get more muscles.

This is a rookie mistake. It might be possible that you have to bring your programming up a notch to meet up with your new muscles.

Here are some intermediate mistakes that might be holding you back:

- Your Rep Range Hasn't Changed

One debate that continues to hold true inside the fitness world is that muscle growth can only be maximized within a rep range of 6 to 12 for each set. Even though this theory has actually been backed by research, but the evidence still hasn't been completely conclusive. But for the sake of arguments, we'll say that doing moderate reps would be best to go up a size. This isn't saying that you need to ONLY train in this narrow rep range.

If you train in the lower rep range like one to five reps for each set will maximize your strength development. This will further your ability to use weights that are heavier during your rep training. By doing this, you will create more tension in your muscles, and this will lead to more growth. Higher reps like 15 to 20 for each set will help increase your lactate threshold.

When you can train your body to delay building up lactic acid, you are going to keep fatigue away when you are training within the 6 to 12 rep stage. This will increase the time under tension, which is just another aspect of growing your muscles.

How can you fix this? Developing your optimal muscles can be achieved by using the entire spectrum of rep ranges. Divide up your program so that it gets built around a moderate rep protocol. You have to make sure to train in both the high and low rep ranges.

Even though several different programs will work, but I've gotten the best gains when I started with lower reps and follow them with high reps and finish off in the 6 to 12 rep stage.

If you can properly do this, this will create a "super-compensation effect" so that you will be able to maximize your muscle gains and see a big difference once you finish training.

- Doing The Same Exercises All The Time

Anyone who goes to the gym regularly will have a few favorite exercises that they do all the time. Even though it is fine to use these old standbys, you shouldn't constantly do them in place of other movements.

When you change up your exercise routine, it has many important benefits for building muscles. It can prevent the "repeated-bout effect" where your muscles get used to the same movements, and this makes them resistant to trauma. Getting rid of this habit can help you increase muscle fibers. This type of damage is what encourages muscle growth.

Muscle fibers aren't actually in the whole length of your muscles. There are different nerve branches in there too. When you change up your exercise routine, you will be hitting everything, so everything gets worked.

Look at it like this. Some people like redheads, others like brunettes, and still others prefer blondes. Your muscles are a greedy bunch and like all of them. In order to keep them growing and happy, you have to give them everything they want. Even the slightest of variations in the exercise routine will work muscles slightly different, and this will enhance results.

How can you fix this? You can use a variation of different exercises throughout your training cycle. This will be accomplished by changing up foot and hand spacing, planes of movement, training angles, and changing modalities.

If you do dumbbell curls, and you usually hold the handle with your little finger resting against an end of the bell, to change that up, do them with your thumb pressing against the bell. This slightest of shifts will work the biceps totally different.

There are endless possibilities. There aren't any hard rules as to how soon your exercises need to be changed up, but the best guideline is once a month.

- Too Little or Too Much Isolation

When talking about exercise selection, there are two different thoughts. One will preach the only way of gaining muscles is by doing big lifts like rows, presses, deadlifts, and squats. The other one says the key to building muscles is by isolating muscles with extensions, curls, and flies.

So which one is right? Actually, they both are.

This isn't a debate since these movements are very complementary. Doing multi-joint exercises uses many muscles and is great for putting on more muscles. Single-joint lets you target specific muscles or even a portion of that muscle. This will enhance your overall symmetry and growth. Try to include a mix of movements so you can improve the symmetry and size of your muscles.

How can I fix this? You need to change up your routine to include both single-joint and multi-joint exercises. Each workout needs to contain at least a couple of "big lifts" and one single-joint movement.

Even when you are working like this, realize that you can't actually isolate specific muscles. Our bodies are designed so that many muscles will constantly be working during any type of movement.

- You Follow Straight Sets

Normal resistance training involves you doing straight sets. This means you do one set, you rest, and then you do another set. You continue doing this for every exercise within your workout.

There isn't anything wrong with this approach. Doing straight sets needs to be a part of your routine foundation. After you have built that foundation, you can mix things up some by doing specialized movements if you want to continue to grow.

How can you fix this?

1. Heavy Negatives: Do eccentric actions at a weight that is greater than you one rep maximum.

2. Dropsets: Do one set until your muscles fail with a load. Immediately reduce the load and continue to train until you fail again.

3. Supersets: Do one exercise and immediately follow it with another without resting in between.

These variations can be great additions to your workout routine. They can create more metabolic stress that will take your muscle growth to new heights.

You can select which ones you want to add to your routine but do this with caution. These techniques need to be thought of as advanced training strategies. Most people make the mistake of pushing themselves too hard, too fast. Because they have a demanding nature, it increases the amount of recovery time that you are going to need. If you don't get that amount of time, you might move into overtraining.

Train hard, but limit how much muscular-overload techniques you do. Just do a few over the course of a program.

- Too Much Cardio

Most people have a goal to increase their muscle development while trying to reduce the level of body fat. How you approach, this seems rather logical. Trying to accelerate the loss of fat, they try to do more cardio while still doing resistance training. They add one level of intensity on top of another level of intensity. They don't leave any room for recovery, and they can't figure out why their body feels as if it is getting weaker instead of stronger.

Don't misunderstand what I'm saying here. Adding aerobic training on a muscle-building routine isn't a bad thing. But when you overdo it, then it becomes a problem. How you switch up aerobic and resistance training are a bit contradictory.

How can you fix this? If you want to maximize your muscles, try to keep the cardio at a moderate level. How do you know how much is too much? This actually depends on you. Some people are able to tolerate more than others.

One guideline is to limit cardio to about three or four times a week that only last 30 to 40 minutes. You could also do two to three high-intensity interval-training routines each week will be great for most bodybuilders. You just need to make sure that you keep in tune with your body and notice any signs that you might be overtraining.

Here are some signs that you might be overtraining:

1. You have a constantly elevated blood pressure and heart rate.

2. You have problems with your stomach.

3. You have drastic changes in your energy levels, emotions, and mood.

4. You have disturbances in your sleep, like insomnia.

Simultaneous weight loss and muscle gain are more effective when you are new at lifting weights and have a significant amount of weight you need to lose. It will be difficult after you have been training for several years.

After you aren't a beginner any longer, the best route is to focus on just one goal at a time.

Chapter 7: Pre-Workout Nutrition

The best foods for you to eat before you exercise all depend on your goals and the kind of workout you like to do. Foods that are protein-rich could help you build muscle while doing resistance training.

When you are trying to figure out a meal to eat before you workout, it's important to find a balance of all the right macronutrients. These are dietary compounds that our bodies need in fairly large quantities to be able to function properly.

There are three macronutrients, and these macronutrients are:

- Fats

- Carbohydrates

- Protein

Macronutrients are the body's key sources for energy; every one of them could contribute something different to your pre-workout meal.

Fats

Fats are a good source of energy for our bodies. Normally, health professionals have told their patients that eating meals that are high in fats before exercising will hurt the body because our bodies will digest than fats slower than it does carbs. This means our bodies can't break down and absorb the fats before a workout.

- Do Fats Help Workouts?

Before you workout, it might be best to eat meals that focus on carbs and proteins rather than fats. It is important to incorporate healthy fats at other times within your diet.

You have to understand that all fats are healthy for you. There are some types like trans and saturated fats could impact your overall health negatively.

- Healthy Fats

Since fat became demonized, people began to eat more processed foods, refined carbs, and more sugar. Because of this the whole world has gotten sicker and fatter. But times do change and studies show that fats aren't the demon it was once thought to be. All the foods that contain fat have been given the status of "superfood." The other kinds of fats are very nutritious. Unsaturated fats can give you several health benefits. Here are some foods that are high in unsaturated fats:

91

- Olive oil: This healthy fat is rich in monounsaturated fats. This is the most used ingredient in the Mediterranean diet. This oil has many health benefits. It contains the Vitamins K and E and is full of powerful antioxidants. These antioxidants can help fight inflammation and can keep the LDL in the blood from getting oxidized. It has all kinds of benefits related to the risk of heart disease. It can improve cholesterol markers and lower blood pressure. It can reduce inflammation and could be helpful on some genes that have been linked to cancer. It is full of antioxidants that help reduce the risk of developing chronic diseases.

- Seeds: Seeds have all the beginning materials that are needed to develop a complex plant. Due to this fact, they are very nutritious. Seeds are a wonderful source of fiber. They also have polyunsaturated fats, monounsaturated fats along with antioxidants, minerals, and vitamins. Seeds could help reduce blood pressure, cholesterol, and blood sugar. The healthiest seeds you can consume: flaxseeds, chia seeds, hemp seeds, sesame seeds, pumpkin seeds, and sunflower seeds.

- o Nuts: Nuts are a great source of protein, fiber, and fat. The fat found in nuts is monounsaturated fat along with omega-3 and omega-6. Studies show people who eat nuts are normally healthier and have a low risk of different diseases. These include type 2 diabetes, heart disease, and obesity. Nuts also have many minerals and vitamins, including Vitamin E and magnesium. The best ones to consume are peanuts, Macadamia nuts, almonds, walnuts, hazelnuts, Brazil nuts, pecans, cashews, and pistachios.

- o Avocados: This fruit is a lot different from most fruits because it is loaded with fats rather than carbs. Avocados are about 77 percent fat. This delicious fruit contains monounsaturated fats known as oleic acid. This is the same fatty acid that is found in olive oil. Avocados are a great source of potassium. It contains 40 percent more than bananas. They also have a small amount of polyunsaturated and saturated fat. They are a great source of fiber. Studies show they can lower triglycerides and LDL cholesterol while raising the HDL cholesterol levels. Although avocados are high in calories and fat, people who eat them usually weightless and will have less belly fat than people who don't eat them. Incorporating avocados into your diet can help reduce the risk of heart disease.

- o Coconut Oil and Coconuts: These are the best sources of saturated fats in the world. People who eat a large amount of coconuts are in great health and don't have heart disease. The fats in coconuts are different than other fats and consist of medium-chain fatty acids. These acids go straight into the liver, where they get turned into ketone bodies. These can help you lose belly fat and could benefit people who have Alzheimer's disease.

- o Dark Chocolate: This is one of those rare foods that really taste great. It is high in fat. It also contains fiber, manganese, copper, magnesium, and iron. It is full of antioxidants and even outranks blueberries. These antioxidants can protect LDL cholesterol and lowers blood pressure. People who consume dark chocolate five or more times each week don't have problems with heart disease as compared to people who don't eat it at all. It can also protect your skin from sun damage and improve your brain function. Be sure you choose dark chocolate that has at least 70 percent cocoa.

- When to Eat Before a Workout

Normally a person needs to eat meals that are high in proteins and complex carbs about two to three hours before you exercise. If you wait a couple of hours after you eat before working out allows the body time to digest what you ate.

You could also eat a smaller meal of simple carbs. If you decide to do this, you will only need to wait about 30 minutes before you work out.

Carbohydrates

These are a much-needed source of energy. Eating the correct amount of carbs before working out will make sure your body has all the energy it needs to work well.

This works best for people who like doing resistance and cardiovascular exercises and other types. Different kinds of carbs will have different impacts on the body:

1. Complex carbs: This would be things like starch and fiber. They give a slower, longer energy source. Whole-grain foods are the best source of complex carbs.

2. Simple carbs: This would be sugars that give you a quick burst of energy. A good source would be white bread.

- Which Carbs are Better to Eat Before Exercising?

Complex carbs have many advantages like:

1. Foods that are complex carbs will be lower on the glycemic index than foods that contain simple carbs. Any kind of food that has a low glycemic index score will cause your blood glucose levels to spike, and this can increase your risk of getting type 2 diabetes.

2. Complex carbs are food compounds that are normally nutrient-rich like beans. Simple carbs are normally food components that don't have any nutritional value like cake and candy.

3. Simple carbs are energy sources that are always short term. If your meal before your workout has too many simple carbs, you might not have enough energy to get through your workout. Complex carbs will give you more consistent energy for a longer period of time.

Our bodies will digest complex carbs slower than simple carbs. To increase the amount of energy before you exercise, you need to eat complex carbs about two to three hours before you workout. Simple carbs need to be eaten about 30 minutes before.

- Complex Carb Sources

Here are some examples of healthy complex carb sources:

1. Whole-grain breads: Every grain is a source of complex carbs. Whole grains are healthier since they include nutrients like magnesium, potassium, and selenium. About half of your grains need to come from sources of whole grains. Fortified whole grains will have iron, folic acid, thiamin, riboflavin, and niacin in them.

2. Oats: If you begin your day by eating oatmeal, continue with this healthy habit. Oats gives your brain and body the fuel it needs along with other important nutrients. All oats aren't created equal, so read the label before you buy to make sure you are getting the most nutrition possible.

3. Brown rice: This is a whole grain that hasn't been as processed as white rice. One serving of brown rice can give you the following nutrients: selenium, manganese, copper, zinc, phosphorus, magnesium, iron, Vitamin B5, Vitamin B6, niacin, thiamin, protein, fat, and fiber.

4. Lentils: Lentils give our bodies a good dose of complex carbs. They are full of nutrients like molybdenum, copper, iron, Vitamin B6, zinc, phosphorus, and folate. Folate can help the production of red blood cells, among other benefits.

5. Beans: This is a great way to get your complex carbs. It doesn't matter if they are garbanzo, pinto, black, white, or kidney, beans are going to give you a lot of fiber.

6. Whole grain pasta: This is high in phosphorus, copper, selenium, manganese, and fiber. If you get the pasta that has been enriched, you will also get B vitamins and iron.

7. Sweet potatoes: These pretty orange veggies give you fiber and beta-carotene. Sweet potatoes can make you feel like you are indulging while doing great things for your body.

8. Broccoli: Kids love to push these "little trees" around on their plate, but broccoli is a very nutritious vegetable. Broccoli is a member of the cruciferous family that includes turnips, rutabaga, collard greens, cabbage, bok choy, Brussels sprouts, cauliflower, and kale. These little powerhouses give you lots of nutrients for only a few calories.

9. Spaghetti Squash: Most people will eat spaghetti squash when they want to cut back on their intake of carbs. Eating spaghetti squash can give you a large portion with only a few carbs and calories but with a lot of nutrients and fiber. If you aren't a fan of substituting spaghetti squash for spaghetti noodles, you could mix it half and

half. Use half spaghetti squash and half whole wheat noodles.

Fruits can give you a good source of simple carbs before you exercise. Bananas are a great choice because they give you simple carbs along with potassium.

Proteins

Proteins give our bodies amino acids and are needed for many bodily functions like building, maintaining and repairing muscle fibers. Consuming meals that contain a decent amount of lean protein before you work out can help improve your performance.

- Whey Protein is a Good Food to Eat Before Working Out

Protein increases how much muscle mass is gained during resistance training. Intense rounds of resistance training can damage your muscles, but eating protein can increase how many amino acids are in the body. These work to stimulate growth, synthesize muscle proteins, and reduce deterioration.

Eating 20 to 30 grams of protein right before exercising could cause muscle protein synthesis to get faster, and that can last for many hours.

- High Protein Sources

Here are some examples of healthy food sources that are high in protein:

1. Soy: Soy is very versatile. It doesn't matter if it is in the form of edamame beans, tempeh, or tofu. This powerful food gives you cardiovascular benefits. It can also protect against osteoporosis, decreases hot flashes for menopausal women, and it can help to prevent colon and prostate cancer.

2. Lentils: These are great sources of potassium, folic acid, and fiber. Consuming this food can reduce your bad cholesterol. Lentils can add fiber, minerals, and vitamins to your diet.

3. Beans: Beans contain amino acids. Amino acids can help build muscles. There are many different types of beans, and they have to be cooked in order to be safe to eat. All types of beans contain folate. Some symptoms of not getting enough folate include irritability, loss of appetite, heart palpitations, fatigue, or weakness. Beans provide these important nutrients: fiber, magnesium, iron, and zinc.

4. Nuts: Nuts are a great source of fats, fiber, and protein. High protein nuts include cashews, chia seeds, sesame

seeds, flax seeds, sunflower seeds, pistachios, almonds, peanuts, pumpkin seeds, and hemp seeds.

5. Spirulina: This "superfood" when eaten with seeds, nuts, oats, and grains will form a complete protein. You can add spirulina powder to your next smoothie.

6. Quinoa: This whole grain is getting very popular these days. Most people cook and eat quinoa seeds like they do most grains. The actual quinoa plant is similar to spinach and beetroots. You can actually eat the leaves and seeds of this wonderful plant.

7. Chia Seeds: These little beauties are full of antioxidants, zinc, calcium, and iron. Because they create a gel when you mix them with water, they make a great substitute for eggs in a recipe. They are also great in smoothies and puddings.

8. Hemp: Many people consider this to be a miracle plant. It is rich in omega-3 and omega-6. They can help with digestion problems and lowers your risk of developing heart disease. Hemp can relieve symptoms of menopause and PMS. One tablespoon of hemp protein powder has 15 grams of protein. This is almost one-third of your daily value.

9. Pumpkin Seeds: Roasting pumpkin seeds with a light sprinkling of salt is a great snack to have available when needed.

10. Peanut Butter: Adding peanut butter to a piece of whole-grain toast makes a great snack. It's great when a favorite snack becomes a source of complete protein.

If you are interested in muscle gain, you need to make sure that you get a decent intake of protein. Research shows that eating between 1.6 to 1.8 grams of protein for each pound of bodyweight is great for building muscle. Most sources recommend that you eat more, but any extra protein won't make any major impact on muscle mass.

Chapter 8: Post-Workout Nutrition

You have just finished a great workout, and you are trying to figure out what you should eat. Read on. In this chapter you are going to learn what would be the best things for you to eat after your workout.

You aren't going to need a resource manager to know the most valuable resource you have is time. You know that there is only a small amount to go around. If you are above average on intelligence, you are going to find ways to get the best return on your investment of time.

This might be recognized and then applied in most aspects of life. It does confuse me why many people ignore this fact when it comes to their exercise routines. From the things I see when I'm at the gym daily, it is very clear that many people who spend time at the gym are just wasting their investment. They spend hours engaging in endurance and strength training programs that only give them little or no results at all.

Do you need some proof? How long has it been since you have seen anybody at your gym make any noticeable progress on their bodybuilding? Better yet, how long has it been since you've made any decent progress on your exercising? Bodybuilding has the potential to give you large returns at any time you can give it.

It is shameful that many people won't ever see any massive difference in their return.

In spite of this reality that is very disappointing, I will tell you that all hope isn't lost. There is a great way for you to capitalize on any investment. Your exercise routine isn't the problem at all. The problem is people don't invest in the other commodity that, when you combine it with exercise will give you the largest return.

They are buying a cart but not a horse. They buy a lemonade stand but don't buy lemons. They spend all their time focused on just their exercise program while completely ignoring how important good nutrition is to the entire program.

The most important part of any exercise routine is eating nutritionally after your workout. Knowing how to eat at this time will make your efforts better while yielding the largest return on your investment.

The Post Workout Period and Remodeling

Both endurance and strength training can bring many aesthetic and health benefits. Exercise by itself is a huge physiological stressor. Some of the symptoms of this stress are normally mild and could include an increased appetite, extra sleep, and muscle soreness.

The symptoms are telling us that all the exercise has caused some damage, the fuel sources for the muscles have been depleted, and the muscles need to be repaired and replenished. Even though the words damage and depletion might sound very negative, they aren't if they are only around for a short time. These types of changes let the muscles adapt by doing better as the exercise puts demands on them.

If you have been doing endurance exercises, your muscles will get damaged and depleted in a very short time, but on the upside, they are building themselves up to be turned into a better machine. If you love strength training, you are going to break down the weaker muscle fibers to build up stronger, bigger ones.

In every case, exercise basically tears down less adapted and old muscle to rebuild muscles that are more functional. This is called remodeling.

Even though remodeling is a lot more complex than anyone could describe, it is important that you know that remodeling will only happen if the muscles are given the correct materials to work with.

If you want to remodel your house, you can hire people to tear down some walls, clean up that mess, and then rebuild the structure better than what was torn down. If I don't provide these people with the right materials, how are they going to do anything? If I don't provide them all the materials they need, all you are going to have is a house with walls.

This holds true with remodeling your muscles. During your exercise routine and right after it, the exercise will break down your carb stores and your protein structures. Your immune system comes to the rescue to clean up this mess.

Then, your body will generate signals that tell your body to begin rebuilding itself. If you don't have the correct carbs and protein, the body can't rebuild. Your muscles won't ever reach their full potential.

My hope is that by using this analogy, it becomes obvious to you that during the time right after the exercise isn't a time to ignore. You have just spent a large amount of time breaking down your muscles for good reasons. You want your body to get more adapted for demands in the future.

In order for you to realize a full return on your investment, you have to give your body the correct raw materials that it needs, mostly carbs and protein.

Feeding Muscles that are Hungry

As stated above, it doesn't matter whether you are female or male and it doesn't matter what type of exercise you do, you have to take your nutrition after your workout seriously and give your muscles the right materials it needs. Since every types of exercise will use carbs for energy, depleting muscle carbs is going to happen. Therefore having a meal the is high in carbs is needed after your workout to refill your energy stores and the carbs in your muscles.

But just any amount of carbs isn't going to work. You have to consume enough carbs to cause a decent amount of insulin to be released. Insulin is a hormone that is responsible for moving amino acids and carbs into your muscles. By doing this, carb resynthesis gets faster, and protein balances get positive, and this leads to the rapid repair of your muscles.

When you eat large amounts of carbs, you will promote large amounts of insulin to be released, which increases glycogen to be stored, and will increase the repair of protein. Research shows that consuming carbs between .8 to 1.2 grams for one kilogram of body weight will accelerate protein repair and maximize glycogen synthesis. If you haven't had a long, intense workout consuming 1.2 grams might be too many carbs. Eating too many carbs could cause them to be changed into body fat.

I personally recommend .8 grams to help speed up muscle carb replenishment while keeping excess fat gain at bay.

Because muscle protein gets degraded while you exercise, adding a large amount of protein to your meal after you workout is needed to help rebuild the muscle's structure. Once you are through exercising, the body will decrease how fast protein gets synthesized and will increase how fast it breaks down protein. Adding some amino acids and protein can reverse this trend, decreases the breakdown of proteins, and increases protein synthesis.

Researchers have tried between .2 and .4 grams of protein for each one kilograms of body weight to show how effective by adding protein to your carb drink after your workout. Increasing the consumption of amino acids might lead to a better protein balance adding .4 grams would be better for your body.

Even though your meal after your workout needs to be rich in carbs and proteins, it needs to be free of any fats. Consuming essential fats is the most overlooked area of our nutritional intake daily, but consuming fats during the time right after you have exercised could decrease how effective your beverage is after you have exercised. Because fat will slow down while traveling through your stomach, eating it after your workout could slow down your digestion along with the absorption of proteins and carbs.

Your meal after you have exercised needs to promote the fastest delivery of protein and carbs to your muscles; this means you need to stay away from fats at this time.

One other important factor is when you need to eat this meal. It is critical that you eat your meal right after you have exercised. As stated above, after you have exercised, your muscles are depleted and need more carbs and protein. Plus, your muscles are "primed" for taking in nutrients.

This is normally called the "window of opportunity." During this recovery period, this window will slowly close. If you don't eat right after you exercise, you are ruining your chances of having a complete recovery. To show how fast this window will close, research shows that eating a meal right after you have exercised is better than eating an hour later.

Eating one hour later is better than eating three hours later. If you wait entirely too long, protein repair and glycogen replenishment gets compromised.

When you made the decision to begin working out, you made the decision to set aside a certain time each week to make yourself physically better. If you haven't thought about your post-exercise nutrition, you will be missing out on all the benefits that exercise gives you.

After you begin paying attention to this variable, your gym time will be invested a lot better.

Nutritional Supplementation Vs. Whole Foods

Standing on top of their soapbox, nutritionists have always stated that whole foods are better than supplemental nutrition. I have just one thought for them:

To quote Oscar Wilde: "Always... it is a meaningless word."

Even though I believe that unprocessed, untreated, unbleached, and complete whole foods need to form the basis of all nutritional regimens. There might be times where supplements could be better than whole foods. When talking about meals after exercising, liquid supplements are better than whole foods for these reasons:

- Liquid Meals Give you Better Nutrients

During the time right after your workout, certain nutrients will speed up your recovery. These include a lot of water, carbs that are on the high end of the glycemic index, and amino acids in certain ratios. It would be best to stay away from fats at this time. The only way to make sure that you get these nutrients in the right amounts is to create a certain liquid blend. Whole foods are going to miss this mark.

- Liquid Meals will Use the "Window of Opportunity."

How quickly the carbs and protein get to your muscles, the better the chances are for building muscles and recovery. Research has shown that people who receive nutrients in the first hour after working out will recover faster than people who wait for three hours after you have exercised. Liquid nutrition just makes more sense.

- Liquid Meals Absorb Faster

Research has shown that liquid supplements that contain carbs and a fast-digesting protein get absorbed faster than eating whole foods.

To help you understand this better, a liquid after workout meal can be completely absorbed between 30 minutes to one hour. This gives your muscles more nourishment during this time. A solid meal could take between two and three hours to completely reach your muscles.

- Liquid Meals are Digestible and Palatable

Normally after an intense workout, many people will complain that eating a large meal is too hard. This is completely understandable because exercise stress can cause your hunger centers to shut down. It is crucial that you eat if you want your muscles to be remodeled, recover from exercising, or to make your muscles larger.

Liquid supplemental formulas are palatable, dense in nutrients, and easy to consume. This provides you will all the nutrition you are going to need during this time. Because these formulas are simple, your gastrointestinal tract won't have any problems processing them. Your stomach is going to thank you for this.

Recommendations

If you do intense training or workouts, begin by consuming 15 grams of protein and 30 grams of carbs in 500 ml of water for every hour you worked out. You could drink on this during your workout or have it right after your workout.

You can find a premixed drink that has quick digesting proteins and carbs, or you can make your own drink. When you have completed your workout, try to eat a complete meal within one hour.

If your main priority is to lose body fat, you need to only consume branched-chain amino acids. Use about fine to 15 grams for every hour you train. If you are already lean, but you still want to lose fat, try for a smaller dose such as a half dose carb to protein combination or just use branched-chain amino acids.

Combining amino acids and carbs during and after exercise can cause a stimulatory effect of testosterone and growth hormones that won't happen for the remainder of the day. Basically, if you drink a protein / carb drink when you are sitting around all day, it isn't going to have the same effect.

When you are picking out your carbs, remember that glucose gets absorbed faster than fructose does. Drinks high in fructose can cause higher cortisol levels, greater fatigue, and gastrointestinal distress.

It could be helpful to add some creatine to your nutrition, too.

Essential amino acids could be more important to help promote a positive nitrogen balance after your workouts.

Chapter 9: Supplements

One common misconception is you need to eat huge amounts of meat if you want to build body mass. If you take the correct supplements and follow a good vegan diet, you will be able to enjoy gains. Keep reading to find out how you can bulk up while staying away from dairy and meat products.

- Eat the Foods that You Like

It can be tough following a vegan diet if you have to choke down what you eat. You need to make sure you are eating foods that you truly enjoy. Try different types of cuisine, such as Indian food. They have fantastic vegan options.

- Consume Many Little Meals

For you to keep a good nitrogen balance while following a vegan diet, you have to have a steady flow of nutrients like carbs, calories, healthy fats, and proteins constantly coming into your body. While supplements can help you do this, you should be eating almost constantly, especially days when you have been training and burning a lot of fuel.

Rather than following the normal three meals a day, eat between six and eight small meals or large snacks during your day. These should come at about every two or four hours. This can keep banana or apple are great choices. Once you have finished exercising, enjoy something healthy and light, such as hummus and some veggies.

- Omega-3s

Omega-3 fatty acids can help you avoid injuries, lose fat, and build muscle. Some bodybuilders who aren't vegan will take fish oil supplements to give their omega-3 intake a boost. This isn't an option for vegans. You need to eat lots of flaxseed oil or powder. Flax seeds are full of lignans, fiber, and omega-3s.

- Consume Beverages that are Healthy

Even though there isn't anything wrong with drinking your favorite beverages every now and then, it is important that you drink healthy beverages when you can. Smoothies made from veggies and fruit are great when you take your supplements. If it is time for a lighter drink, try natural juice, tea, or water rather than soda.

- Consume Healthy Carbs

Eating carbs can help you build muscle. Bad news is that all carbs aren't equal. You need to consume low-glycemic carbs that have lots of fiber like oatmeal, black beans, chickpeas, lentils, barley, pasta, and whole wheat breads.

- Eat More Calories

It isn't a secret that eating vegan normally means that you are consuming fewer calories. If you want to build mass, you are going to need a diet that includes more calories than a normal vegan diet. If you don't get enough calories, your body might begin to use itself as a source of energy, and this can cause you to lose mass.

Other than taking supplements, you need to eat foods that are heavy on calories like whole-wheat breads, raisins, quinoa, and nuts. You can also consume coconut oil or peanut butter to some of your foods to boost their number of calories. You could also drink some smoothies that are rich with calories by adding some soy milk.

- Vegan Supplements

If you want to build muscle, you need to consume lots of protein. Even though meat is the normal source of protein, you can get protein from tofu, beans, vegetables, or other meat substitutes that have lots of protein. Just eating foods that are rich in protein isn't normally enough to put on any mass.

Adding whey protein powder is normal within the fitness community, but bad news whey is not vegan. Whether you eat a vegan diet or whey protein upsets your stomach, there are some supplements that can boost your protein intake a lot.

You can find began protein powder that has a balanced blend of pumpkin seed protein, watermelon seed protein, and organic pea protein that gives you 20 grams of protein for 110 calories. It is non-allergenic, gluten-free, organic, non-GMO, and vegan. It is perfect for anyone who has a sensitive stomach or any dietary restrictions.

Even though you need to be meticulous about your eating, you want to enjoy life. The right supplements will go a long way to help boost your gains. Never be afraid to change up your diet to keep things exciting and fun.

Testosterone is normally created inside the Leydig cells in men. How much it makes gets regulated by a luteinizing hormone.

There are many vitamins and minerals that can influence how much testosterone gets produced. The important ones are vitamin D, magnesium, and zinc.

Everyone of these has a role in producing testosterone, and a deficiency in just one could cause a disturbance in the process, and this could cause a drop in the levels.

If you tried to make up all these deficiencies with supplements, you would be taking over 100 pills each day. Yes, you could do this, but there isn't any need to. Except for a few exceptions, most of these deficiencies can be fixed by changing up your diet.

Vitamin D3 is the main one that could be a huge problem. It is hard to get enough with food, and if you don't live on a sunny beach, it will be impossible to get enough through exposure to the sun. For this main reason, you need to take a supplement.

Nobody can talk about testosterone without talking about sleep and exercise. Compound, heavy exercises have been known to create an anabolic effect on your body while growth hormone and testosterone get synthesized and then released when you get a good quality of sleep.

When you can combine all this with the food you eat, these are the things you have to do to fix it if you want your testosterone levels really soar.

Let's look at some natural foods that you need to eat if you want to boost your testosterone:

- Celery

Celery has many health benefits. It prevents muscular degeneration and can improve your eye health. It can reduce the pain and swelling in joints. Celery can prevent UTIs in women. It can reduce cholesterol and blood pressure levels. It can improve immunity and prevents cancer. Celery can help you get relief from asthma and migraines. It can promote better cardiovascular health. It can manage the symptoms of diabetes. Celery is a good way to get Vitamin K. If you love green shakes, more than likely you put it in them. If you haven't considered it before, you need to think about it.

First and foremost, celery is high in Vitamin K. This help keep the best levels of testosterone. Just one cup can give you one-quarter of your daily recommended intake.

Androstenol and androstenone are powerful anabolic hormones that are found in celery. Increasing your intake of celery should have a positive impact on your testosterone levels. Since there isn't any potential for side effects, celery can be something worth looking into.

consume the, and there are many bodybuilders who do, in fact, use them.

Adding raw, uncooked quinoa to smoothies will give you about one third of your daily zinc, 55 percent of your daily magnesium, and 46 percent of your daily folate. Raw, uncooked quinoa is full of minerals and vitamins.

- Avocado

If you don't love avocados or guacamole, here are some reasons you should.

Other than being full of more than 20 vitamins along with copper, magnesium, and zinc, it is a good source of monounsaturated fatty acids. This is what you need to consume if you would like to boost your testosterone levels.

- Fava Beans

These aren't a common food, but they do contain the strongest natural growth hormone supplement L-dopa.

Just a half a gram of L-dopa can increase the circulation of growth hormones. The highest concentration happens one hour after you have eaten them. Other studies show they can increase luteinizing hormones and testosterone.

- Asparagus

Asparagus has nutrients such as Vitamin K, Vitamin B6, magnesium, and D-aspartic acid.

If you haven't ever heard about D-aspartic acid, it can increase your testosterone levels in just a short amount of time. It is great for increasing your fertility.

Ancient Greeks back in the second century used asparagus as an aphrodisiac. Now we know why it actually works.

- Bananas

Bananas might not be at the top of the list of foods you normally eat to increase your testosterone levels, but they should be. They contain bromelain enzyme, potassium, and Vitamin Bs. Bromelain enzymes are normally found in pineapples. This is the thing that causes the biting aftertaste. That is actually the enzymes breaking down the tissues in your mouth. Don't worry; the effects are negligible.

In one study with competitive cyclists, just one gram of bromelain enzymes each day can counteract the effects of endurance exercises on testosterone. The level of testosterone can significantly drop if you do a lot of endurance work. By adding bromelain, athletes don't have to worry about any drops in testosterone levels.

If you do endurance exercises for weight loss or sport, eating pineapple, banana, or supplementing with bromelain is just one way to keep the testosterone levels up.

- Spinach

There are many health benefits to eating spinach. It is full of powerful nutrients like Vitamin D, iron, Vitamin A, and folate. Just like all other leafy greens, spinach gives you calcium, magnesium, and fiber.

Spinach can help strengthen your eyes. It provides anti-aging properties. It is full of omega-3 fatty acids. Spinach contains niacin, folate, riboflavin, Vitamin B1, and Vitamin B6. Spinach is very high in iron. It can help maintain a low blood sugar, prevents constipation, and helps with digestion. Spinach can help your body fight stroke, cardiovascular disease, and atherosclerosis. It can fight wrinkles, acne, and psoriasis. Spinach can lower your blood pressure. Spinach can alkalize your body.

If you know who Popeye is, you know he used spinach's power to get his strength. It doesn't work like that in real life, but it does have extremely high levels of magnesium that has shown to increase testosterone levels.

One study researched how effective a magnesium supplement was on sedentary men and athletes. It found that both had an increase in their testosterone levels. The increase was higher in athletes. It looks like exercise and magnesium are a wonderful combination to help boost your testosterone levels.

Because one package of spinach contains about half of your daily intake of magnesium, it would be best if you took a supplement or add other foods that give you magnesium into your diet, such as pumpkin seeds orchard.

All-Natural Testosterone Boosters

The time that you need to reorganize your diet along with some adjustments won't be anything when the results you get give you a better quality of life, better libido, an energetic life, and a body that is full of muscles.

This list might seem a bit daunting, and this isn't even a total list of the foods that can have an anabolic effect on your body.

Rather than just thinking this is a cool chapter without doing anything to change your diet, write down some of these foods and find out where you can add them into your normal food habits. Grab a banana to have as a delicious snack at work or school. Have a bowl of oats for breakfast to give you a testosterone and protein boost to your day.

Try not to get hung up on anyone food. The main thing is to make sure you are getting enough water and calories to your normal diet along with adequate sleep and exercise. This will become the basis for your success

Chapter 11: Plant-Based Diets for Improved Mood and to Avoid Depression

Depression is usually seen in these terms as extreme symptoms such as sadness, discouragement, discouragement, emptiness, or a lack of value or purpose. It affects many people and can change lives. Although treatment and counselling often help relieve symptoms, lifestyle improvements, such as healthy eating, can also improve human health. However, depression can manifest as physical pain or pain that has no apparent cause, such as unexplained chest pain, muscle aches, tremors, or hot flashes.

Bodybuilder and Depression

It is self-evident and paradoxical that bodybuilders are malnourished until they get sick. Their strange and ceremonial eating behavior is born meaningless, but on a whim, only spread in myths, and is believed to be the need for legitimate and reasonable pre-calculation. Mythical beliefs about what constitutes proper nutrition, attitude, and behavior in some bodybuilders can create a biochemical atmosphere that contributes to the development of depression. Like most diseases, depression can be prevented. It is true that there is a cure. In some cases, there is a complete cure. However, the best option is to avoid depression.

- Make sure your diet is balanced.
- Make sure your diet is enriched with proper vitamins and minerals.
- Avoid the drugs common in some bodybuilding worlds.
- Maintain an entertaining and rewarding lifestyle.
- Avoid unnecessary stress (mental and physical) that is often associated with today's enthusiastic pace.

Symptoms

Depressive symptoms such as mood and anxiety improved sufficiently to meet remission criteria in more than 32% of the participants.

You may further observe exhausted and have trouble sleeping at night. Other symptoms include irritability, anger, and a loss of interest in things that cause pleasure, including sex. Depression can cause headaches, chronic body aches, and pain that may not respond to the drug. It is also a result of certain neurological disorders such as Alzheimer's, epilepsy, and multiple sclerosis.

Depression effect on Digestive system

Depression is often considered a mental illness, but it also plays a vital role in appetite and nutrition. Some people are concerned with overeating or overeating. This can lead to weight gain and obesity-related illnesses such as type 2 diabetes, which can lead to complete loss of appetite and even an inability to eat the right amount of food. When older people suddenly lose interest in eating, a condition known as anorexia nervosa occurs.

Nutritional problems can cause the following symptoms:

- normal
- cramps
- constipation
- Malnutrition

These symptoms may not improve with medication unless the person eats appropriately. Sweets and carbohydrate foods can be instantly soothed, but their effects are only temporary. If you sustain from inflation, it is necessary to eat a healthy diet. Nutrients are essential so that the body's neurotransmitters can fire accurately.

In a total of 21 studies, healthy eating habits were significantly associated with a reduced likelihood of depression. The inclusion of an RCT review is said to provide the most persuasive evidence of a link between eating habits and depression. The mood values of the VEG participants improved significantly after two weeks. One of the factors that can contribute to depression is the person's eating habits, which determine which nutrients to consume. A 2017 research discovered that physiques with modest to difficult unemployment receive nutritional counselling, and their symptoms improve when they eat healthier for 12 weeks. The improved diet focused on nutritious fresh foods and whole foods. Fried foods, including processed, refined grains, candy, and junk food, were also limited.

Diet to Manage Depression

- **Selenium**

Some scientists suggest that increasing selenium intake can improve mood, reduce anxiety, and help treat depression. Selenium is discovered in a diversity of vegetables, including:
Full grain.
Brazil nuts.

- **Vitamin D**

According to a 2019 meta-analysis, vitamin D could help improve depression symptoms.
Humans consume most of the vitamin D from sunlight, but food sources are also relevant.
Foods that can provide vitamin D include:
Improved dairy products.

- **Omega-3 fatty acids**

Absorbing omega-3 greasy hallucinogens can overcome the risk of mood disorders and brain diseases by strengthening brain function and protecting the myelin sheath that protects nerve cells.
Here are some excellent sources of omega-3 fatty acids:
Flax seeds, linseed oil, chia seeds.
Walnuts.

- **Antioxidants**

Vitamin A (beta-carotene), C, and E contain substances known as antioxidants.
Antioxidants help eliminate free radicals, the waste of natural body processes that can accumulate in the body. If the body cannot remove enough free radicals, oxidative stress can occur. Many health problems can arise, such as anxiety and depression. Fresh plant foods like berries are an excellent source of antioxidants. A diet is rich in fresh fruits and vegetables, soy, and other botanical products.

- **Protein**

The organization uses a protein called tryptophan to build serotonin, a "feeling hormone."
Tryptophan occurs in chickpeas.

Avoid Food

Some foods can make depression symptoms worse.

Liquor

There is a distinct connection between palliative and difficult health problems. People can drink alcohol to deal with depression, but alcohol can aggravate or trigger new bouts of depression and anxiety.

Refined Foods

Useful foods like fast food and junk food are high in calories and may contain little nutrients.
Studies indicate that people who consume much fast food are more prone to depression than people who eat almost fresh ingredients. If you suffer from depression, you may want

pretzels, white bread, soda, etc., but studies have shown that an overdose of refined carbohydrates can lead to depression. A review of women without a history of depression, substance abuse, or other mental illness found that consuming refined carbohydrates raised blood sugar and increased the risk of depression.

Processed foods, especially those with a lump of high sugar and refined carbohydrate content, may be at increased risk of depression. When a person eats refined carbohydrates, the body's energy level rises quickly, but then falls. It is best to choose a fresh, nutritious whole food that provides a stable source of energy over time.

Processed Food and Oils

Refined saturated fats can cause inflammation, impair brain function, and worsen symptoms of depression. While soup cans are the easiest way to refuel your body when you are low on energy, you should think twice before grabbing the can opener. In more than 3,000 British studies, people who ate most processed foods had a higher incidence of depression, and those who ate more whole grains had a much lower risk of disease.

Avoid Fats in your diet:

Trans fat, red meat, and processed meat fat are found in many processed foods. Studies with at least one thistle and corn oil rich in omega-6 fatty acids have shown that moderate caffeine in the form of coffee can benefit people with depression. The benefits of caffeine can be due to its irritant and antioxidant properties. Studies examining the link between fatty acid intake or the use of cooking fats and depression in the Mediterranean population have found an unhealthy relationship between the consumption of trans fatty acids and the risk of depression. It is natural to crave depression, salty, and fried foods if you are depressed, but it clearly shows that a healthy diet with lots of whole foods feels good. Instead, limit your healthy meals and ask friends and relatives to create a healthy meal plan immediately.

What foods can help with depression?

Regardless of your nutritional preference, there are a variety of options that can achieve mood-lifting effects. This does not mean that you have to rethink your eating habits and only have to consume these foods. However, knowing what foods affect your mood can help treat depression symptoms.

Although serotonin appears to be involved in depression, its mechanism is complex, and its correct functioning is unknown. However, eating foods that can raise serotonin levels is beneficial, and a whole-grain and productive diet can actually reduce your risk of depression.

Vegan Food

If you don't eat a balanced diet, your vegan diet is anaemic. There was a debate at the time about whether these meals were as healthy as any belief. Similarly, vegetarians tend to suffer from severe eating disorders such as anorexia nervosa and bulimia. This is because foods contain no nutrients that are important for beef. Study says too truncated proteid in the food can affect serotonin and hormone levels, affect mood, lead to optimism and well-being, and can cause anorexia nervosa. More than half of the people diagnosed with the disease say: "Proper vegetarian diet means more than cutting meat." (Vegetarian diet and mental illness) Studies were carried out in Germany, Great Britain, some western countries and India. According to a small group survey, vegetarians may be more likely than non-vegetarians. Was shown. The result was solid. The results explain how vegetarians lose fat and consume healthier fiber. But vegetarians and non-vegetarians are aware of the difference in mental health. Vegetarians can be affected by the vegetarian diet, which is essential for depression, as it removes individual greases important for brain function such as fatty acids and consumes little vitamin B12. The neurological function describes "the nutritional status on a biological level, which can impair the neurological function due to a vegetarian diet" (vegetarianism, mental illness).

Of course, we all know that exercise is a great way to exercise depression, but that's not a very specific recommendation. Let's take a more intimate glimpse at how it works. Not all people with a high body fat percentage are not eligible. However, most people use ultra-fastness as a measure of inactivity, and it is inappropriate to compare it with depression statistics for extensive statistical analysis. She. According to Gabriel Villarreal, strength trainer and licensed therapist with a master's degree in clinical mental health:

"If you are a person, there is a 75% chance that there will be another person, regardless of whether you have depression, ADHD, anxiety, postpartum depression, Alzheimer's or other mental disorders. If diagnosed as disabled, it is with 75% high.

Although neurology is far from fully scientific, we know that dopamine, norepinephrine, and serotonin are three important neurotransmitters that tend to be low in people with depression.
139

Dopamine in particular is the key to the mental reward system and helps motivate people to start and complete their activities. Exercise seems to raise dopamine levels for around 30-90 minutes, but this is a big window, and regular exercise can improve a person's ability to produce hormones throughout the day. Second, there is noradrenaline and serotonin, which are strong in emotions as well as involved in the activity of the nervous system and the sleep cycle. Exercise increases the production of these chemicals, but especially increases the heart rate. Because of this, cardiopulmonary function is often more uplifting than occasional weight sessions. However, a powerful lift drives the stove up and achieves the same effect in a short time. Power foundation has the combined benefit of increasing testosterone and growth hormone. Both low values generally correlate with depression across studies. Training also has important psychological benefits. The first is that you are out of the house and in an environment where you are with others. Fitness improves your social status. Because we perceive individuals as more competent.In summary, do not shortly market the benefits of exercise to prevent or overcome depression. It is a natural, healthy and constructive way to maintain physical and mental health.

Lower Skeletal Muscle

According to a research advertised in the Journal of Affective Disorders, the mass associated with depressive symptoms in men may be independent of the mass associated with depression symptoms in men, not women.The study included 1151 men and 2176 women between the ages of 30 and 64, all of whom completed a questionnaire and adjusted the skeletal muscle mass of the limbs to the size squared (ASM / Ht2). Men in the lower and middle vs. Upper ASM / HT2 tertile showed more symptoms of depression. A gradual decrease of 1 kg / m2 in men strongly correlated with symptoms of depression, but a similar correlation was not observed in women before or after menopause.

Bioelectrical impedance analysis was used to measure the skeletal muscle mass of the limbs, which was assessed as the total mass of all limb muscles. The researchers included both continuous values and tertiary amounts in the analysis. Depression symptoms were categorized using the Beck Depressive Inventory-II. A value of 20 or higher indicates a high level of depressive symptoms.

Limitations of the study included the fact that skeletal muscle mass and symptoms of depression were assessed only once, bioelectrical impedance analysis to determine skeletal muscle mass, cross-sectional study architecture, and measurement of depressive symptoms. The use of self-reporting was used. Health instruction not simply builds muscle, but it also helps fight depression.

- Strength training, also called strength training or strength training, can reduce the symptoms of depression, according to a new meta-analysis of the study.
- Studies show that this form of exercise is almost as effective in treating depression as aerobic exercise.
- According to a new report, this finding will provide healthcare professionals with new ways to fight depression.

Researchers have long known that aerobics can significantly reduce symptoms of depression. (Of course, cardio training also has many positive effects on physical health.) This is an important finding, as this is the first systematic analysis of the highest quality studies that assess the impact of strength training on depression. Also, the types of exercises that researchers say it is important to maintain muscle mass with age show that people benefit from mental health.

Strength training is often referred to as strength training and includes weight exercises such as weight lifting and pushes. We already knew that strength training could strengthen people, build muscle, improve endurance and strength. There is also good evidence that increasing exercise can reduce anxiety.However, scientists did not know whether this type of training could alleviate the symptoms of depression and aerobic exercise.

Therefore, exercise is a remarkable element of the depression supply. Not only are there no adverse side effects, but they also reduce the likelihood of cardiovascular disease, the leading cause of death in the United States (and the leading cause of death in people with major depression). It doesn't automatically heal depression to execution. Some cases are more severe, and some may be less responsive to exercise than others. However, these forms of exercise have at least a moderate impact, which means that they can help

Chapter 12: Okinawa Diet for Healthy Life and Bodybuilding

This thread is about nutrition and how robust nutrition systems can affect our mind and body. Basically, the Okinawa diet is the diet of the Okinawa people. Okinawan diet comes from the word "Okinawa". This is Japan's island with the highest longevity and health in the world

Okinawa is the largest Kikuyu archipelago off the coast of Japan between the East China Sea and the Philippine Sea. Okinawa belongs to one of the five regions of the world known as the Blue Zone. The Blue Zone people live a very long and healthy life compared to the rest of the world that Okinawans enjoy. Although this can be explained by various genetic, environmental, and lifestyle factors, experts believe that one of the most potent effects is diet.

What is the Okinawa Diet?

Okinawan meals are mainly prepared on a plant basis. High fiber carbohydrates are a staple. Think of root vegetables, whole grains, soy products. Other common ingredients are seaweed and seafood. Red meat and processed foods are generally restricted.

In the purest sense, the Okinawan diet refers to the traditional diet of the people who live on the Japanese island of Okinawa. It is believed that their unique diet and lifestyle allow them to live the most extended life on earth. Cooking oil is not very important in Okinawa's diet. The food is steamed, boiled or lightly fried, which effectively removes frequently added fats. The same applies to sugar. The diet focuses on savoury foods, so fewer additional sweeteners are needed.

In addition, the amount of food ingested is remarkable, especially if your customer is considering this weight loss diet. Okinawan usually eat until full. They eat small portions all day long, not the large crowded plates that many Americans consume.

The traditional Okinawan diet is low in calories and fat and high in carbohydrates. In addition to vegetables and soy products, a small amount of pasta, rice, pork and fish is highlighted. In recent years, with the modernization of food production and eating habits, the nutritional content of the diet in Okinawa has changed. Low calorie and mostly carbohydrate-based, but now contains more protein and fat.

The distribution of the main nutrients in the Okinawan diet is summarized in this table (2):

Original modern

145

Carbohydrates 85% 58%

9% protein 15%

Contains 6% fat, 2% saturated fat, 28%, 7% saturated fat.

In addition, the Okinawan culture treats food as medicine and uses many traditional Chinese medical practices. Therefore, diets include herbs and spices that are known to have health benefits, such as turmeric and mugwort. The Okinawa lifestyle also emphasizes daily physical activity and mindful eating habits. The health benefits associated with traditional Okinawan diets have spawned a mainstream version aimed at promoting weight loss. Although this derivative promotes nutrient-rich food intake, it is strongly influenced by the Western diet. An Okinawan diet that is rich in carbohydrates and vegetables refers to the traditional diet and lifestyle of people living in the Japanese islands of Okinawa. Mainstream version promotes weight loss.

Bodybuilding focuses on building the muscles of the body through weight lifting and nutrition. Bodybuilding, whether leisure or competition, is often referred to as a lifestyle because it includes time both inside and outside the gym. To maximize your fitness results, you need to focus on your diet. Eating the wrong food can adversely affect your bodybuilding goals. With careful planning, bodybuilders can not only support their efforts in the gym but also eat in a way that maintains their health.

Foods to Eat

Bodybuilding diets are usually divided into filling and cutting phases. During this phase, the percentage of macronutrients does not change, but calorie intake changes. The food you eat traditionally does not have to be different for the filling and cutting phase. Many of the benefits of the Okinawan diet are due to the ample supply of whole, nutritious, high antioxidant foods. While essential nutrients are essential for the proper functioning of the body, antioxidants protect the body from cell damage. Unlike other Japanese, Okinawans consume very little rice. Instead, sweet potatoes are the primary calorie source, followed by whole grains, legumes, and high-fibre vegetables.

The Staple Foods in a Traditional Okinawan Diet are (2):

Collect green and yellow vegetables. Green leafy vegetables are included in almost every diet, but for a good reason. Rich in nutrition. Yellow vegetables bring carotenoids. This helps reduce inflammation and improve the immune system.

147

Vegetables (58-60%): sweet potato (orange and purple), seaweed, seaweed, bamboo shoot, radish, bitter melon, cabbage, carrot, Chinese okra, pumpkin, blue papaya, pepper.

Cereals (33%): millet, wheat, rice, pasta.

Soy foods (5%): tofu, aroma o, natto, green soybeans.

Meat and seafood (1-2%): all cuts, including mainly white fish, shellfish and sometimes pork organs.

Other (1%): alcohol, tea, spices, soup (soup).

Different versions of tofu, aroma or edamame soybean were incorporated into many Okinawan dishes. Organic soy products are a solid protein option for plant-based nutrition. It is a good source of nutrients and is known to offer some health benefits such as lowering cholesterol. However, soy is not suitable for everyone. Talk to a nutritionist to find the best options for your health.

In addition, jasmine tea is freely consumed in this diet, and spices that are high in antioxidants like turmeric are common. The traditional Okinawan diet consists of very nutritious, mainly plant-based foods, especially sweet potatoes. These foods provide an abundant supply of antioxidants and fibre.

Food to Avoid

As with training, a diet is an essential part of bodybuilding. If you eat the right amount of the right food, your muscles will get the nutrients they need to recover from their workouts and get more prominent and more reliable. Conversely, eating the wrong food or eating the wrong food inadequately leads to poor results.

Here are Foods You Should Focus on and Foods to Limit or Avoid:

Okinawa's traditional diet is quite limited compared to modern western foods. Because Okinawa is relatively isolated, the island's geographic nature has prevented access to a variety of foods for much of its history.

To follow this diet, you need to limit the following food groups:

Meat: processed products such as beef, chicken, bacon, ham, salami, hot dogs, sausages and other sausages.
Animal products: eggs, dairy products, milk, cheese, butter, yogurt, etc.
Processed foods: refined sugar, muesli, breakfast cereals, snacks, processed edible oils.
Legumes: Most legumes other than soy.

149

Other foods: most fruits, nuts, seeds.

The modern mainstream version of the Okinawan diet is more flexible because it is mainly based on calories. Some low-calorie foods like fruit are allowed, but most high-calorie foods like dairy, nuts, and seeds are still restricted.

The Okinawan diet limits or eliminates some groups of foods, including most fruits, meats, dairy products, nuts, seeds, and refined carbohydrates. Due to the geographical isolation of Okinawa, traditional eating styles have historically been restricted.

Health Benefits of the Okinawa Diet:

Although the Okinawan menu has many health benefits, it is often due to its high antioxidant content and high quality, nutritious foods.

Longevity

The most notable benefit of a traditional Okinawan diet is the apparent impact on lifespan. Okinawa is home to people over 100 years who are at least 100 years older than any other region in the world. Proponents of the mainstream version of the diet claim that it also promotes longevity, but there is no substantial research to verify these claims.
Many factors such as genetics and the environment influence the lifespan, but the choice of lifestyle also plays an important role. High content of free radicals - or reactive particles that cause stress and cell damage - can accelerate aging.

Studies show that foods rich in antioxidants can slow down the aging process by protecting cells from free radical damage and reducing inflammation. Traditional Okinawan diets consist mainly of plant foods, have potent antioxidant and anti-inflammatory properties, and can extend their lifespan. Low-calorie, low-protein and high-carbohydrate foods can also promote longevity. Animal studies suggest that reduced-calorie diets, which consist of more carbohydrates and less protein, tend to support a longer lifespan compared to high-protein Western foods. More research is needed to understand better how Okinawa's diet contributes to human longevity.

Reduce the risk of a chronic illness. Not only do people in Okinawa live longer, but they also have less experience with chronic diseases such as heart disease, cancer and diabetes. Diet plays a role because Okinawa foods contain essential nutrients, fibre, and anti-inflammatory compounds, while low in calories, refined sugars, and saturated fats. In a traditional diet, most calories come from sweet potatoes. Some experts even claim that sweet potatoes are one of the healthiest foods to eat. Sweet potatoes provide healthy fibre and have a low glycaemic index (GI), which does not contribute to a rapid rise in blood sugar. Also provides essential nutrients like calcium, potassium, magnesium, vitamins A and C.

In addition, sweet potatoes and other colourful vegetables, which are often consumed in Okinawa, contain potent plant substances, so-called carotenoids. Carotenoids have antioxidant and anti-inflammatory properties and can help prevent heart disease and type 2 diabetes. Okinawan diets also provide relatively high amounts of soy. Studies have shown that certain soy-based foods are associated with a reduced risk of chronic diseases such as certain types of cancer, such as heart disease and breast cancer. Many foods that makeup Okinawa's traditional diet can extend lifespan and reduce the risk of chronic diseases.

many other diets and lifestyles. If you are unsure whether an Okinawan diet will meet your nutritional goals, contact a nutritionist or health care provider and plan a plan that suits your needs.

The Okinawan diet emphasizes various principles of healthy eating and lifestyle, including high vegetable intake. However, some people can be too restrictive or have too many carbohydrates. Meals in Okinawa are based on the food and lifestyle of the islanders in Okinawa, Japan. It emphasizes nutrient-rich, high-fibre vegetables and lean protein sources and discourages saturated fats, sugar and processed foods. Its benefits may include a longer lifespan, but it is restrictive and can have a high sodium content.
Still, modern diets remove some of these restrictions and are geared towards weight loss. Please note that this latest version has not been subjected to rigorous scientific research.
Many of these factors are numerous weight loss recipes when combined with exercise programs. Other recommended health benefits include:

longevity
Reduce the risk of chronic diseases
Reduce inflammation
Conversely, it is known that this diet contains a high sodium content, which is dangerous for some people. In addition, the
155

elimination of most foods from some food groups leaves room for possible malnutrition. If customers are on this diet, be sure to include a variety of vegetables and whole grains that can provide adequate levels of protein, calcium, and other nutrients. The combination of lots of exercise and nutrition enables a balanced approach to fitness and health. There is no diet plan that works for everyone, but there are common themes that touch these and other diets to support a healthy lifestyle for you and your customers.

Be careful about what you eat and how much you eat.
Focus on whole foods and leafy greens.
Stick to lean or vegetable proteins.
Limit sugar, saturated fats, and processed foods.

Chapter 13: What Bodybuilding Demands

Many bodybuilding historians point bodybuilders back to the ancient Greeks and Romans for a full understanding of the evolution of the sport. The Greeks highlighted friendly competition among adjacent countries than to throw a spear to kill a lion or enemy, and the Greeks would measure the distance it could be tossed. Despite swinging a sword, the Greeks competed with competitors. Besides, being deserted for years, the Greek ideals of the sport were revived in 1896 as the modern Olympics.

Gym: The Safety Measures

Before starting into the actual training principles and techniques that encompass the sport of bodybuilding, a brief understanding of gym safety measure needed. If you follow the directions correctly, you would never experience an injury or life-threatening situation while training in the gym. Eventually, safety is the most crucial key, and most gyms would keep the must to follow safety rules set out to ensure it.

First Warm-Up

The immense preponderance of damages is made when somebody sink directly into their most enormous poundage before their fibres are adequately warmed up. Take your muscles as elastic bands. Elastic bands lose their flexibility when cooled. Conversely, they'll stretch better when warmed. Most significantly, never, ever start your workout with your most massive weight!

Where Possible, Take Help In The Gym

Take help in the gym, and you will find spotter, a person who stands next to you, that could potentially leave you stuck under a barbell. Work out such as squats and bench presses should not be done using heavyweight unless you have a trusted help.

Use Collars On Your Barbell Exercises

You can think of collars as bolts to lock the weight plates on the ends of a barbell. Even with the best method, you will generally have a slight angle to the bar, at least during exercise. If the bar slopes too much, the weight plates may slip off to that side, and then the bar will intensely fall in the opposite direction. Subject to the weight and exercise, you could potentially break a wrist, or worse.

Use A Leathered Belt ForWeigh-Lifting

During the exercise, while lifting the weights, you can consider a weightlifting belt as your shin guard or baseball glove. It's like protective gear. Some activities place tremendous strain on the spine. A piece of leather will protect your lower back on such exercises as squats, deadlifts, and various pressing and rowing movements.

Putting Your Weights Back To Their Proper Racks

Placing weights back after exercise on the rack is a time saver for everybody. Otherwise, it gets really annoying when you need weight and time is wasted on finding them in the gym. To enforce this rule, most gym employees get strict, but please take it upon yourself to clean up after your workout.

Never Be Afraid To Ask For Advice

If you have no idea about weights, take the advice of the gym instructors, take benefit of their knowledge anytime you have a bodybuilding-related question. If they are not there, ask gym members, save time and yourself from muscle strains.

Use Good Technique

Do the exercises using proper techniques, because you are using weights on your body muscles, so following useful techniques would bring positive results that will motivate you further.

Wipe Down Your Bench After Use

When you are done with your reps, exercise than wipe out your sweat because human sweat carries hundreds of germs. It gets disgusting to go to a bench or machine and see a layer of someone else's sweat dripping all over it!

Wear The Proper Outfit

Gyms can be very strict about the outfit, and most fitness centres will leave it up to the members. In terms of the sneaker, always have a good pair of sneakers. Exercises will put a great deal of stress on your ankles, and you will require reliable assistance to protect the small muscles and bones in this region.

Never Stop Learning

Always learn from the mistakes you make in the gym, the fact reading this book is the first step, and move on further from the instructors to fellow gym peers.

Even the greatest seek medical advice!

Do not be reluctant to go to the doctor and seeking medical expertise because you are in the middle of making your body and asking medical advice will let you understand where your organization stands, and what further is required.

Genetic Marker – Bone Size

For saying, there is a direct relationship between bone size and muscle bulk. A small-boned individual will have far more difficulty developing the muscle size as a larger-boned individual. Exceptionally large-boned bodybuilders may have more muscle mass, but they often appear blocky and chunky. Small boned individuals tend to exhibit far better proportions and symmetry.

Hormonally Stimulated

An important variable that can affect muscle size is hormone levels, especially testosterone. Sufficient, those who have a naturally high level of the male hormone testosterone are likely to have more muscle mass than those who have a low level. High testosterone levels are one of the main reasons why men are on average taller and more muscular than women. Anyone who uses a healthy hormone system will not only carry weight but also attack! You can use energy and energy sparingly. Studies

161

have shown that performing basic complex exercises like squats, deadlifts, and bench presses can increase natural testosterone levels.

Muscle Size And Muscle Bulk

While hardness and structure od, the muscle size and bulk are relevant, bodybuilding is about muscles, resilient, massive, robust muscles! The granted scale is often related to height and bone structure.

Symmetry, Balance And Proportion Of The Body

It's not sufficient enough to just have huge muscles; the muscle mass must be equally distributed over the body. Top to bottom, from one side to another, your organization must be evenly balanced and proportioned. Eventually, the goal is to have your body shaped as stable as the Greek statues.

Muscular Definition

Now, bodybuilders are anticipated to keep as little body fat as possible. If your muscles don't display patterns and cross patterns, you can find your self in a very typical condition of losing motivation, strength. If competing, you will be anticipating to lose.

Vascular Signs

The term refers to how bright the veins are in the bas-reliefs of your body. For some bodybuilders, the threads are closer to the surface; for others, they are more profound. Some bodybuilders have excellent vascular density.

Muscle Separation

Muscle separation or muscle split-up refers to how well muscles are split-up from one another. It also refers to how clear the subparts of the muscles stand out from one another. To keep your self really on edge, your muscles should not appear as one large lump of mass.

Level Of High Energy

Building a good-looking, highly vigour, and with a higher level of energy, physique takes at least a few months. Muscular bodybuilders will require an investment on the body of years of high-intensity workouts. Bodybuilders with the stamina and vitality to endure such physical exertion will survive.

Metabolism A Must Keep

One of the absolute necessities of bodybuilding is to keep a healthy metabolism. A great-looking figure means being able to eat a lot of healthy foods and have it evolved into muscle, not fat. Some bodybuilders can eat more than 5,000 calories per day and still keep a six-pack set of abdominals.

Will Power

You need to be very persistent and have strong will powers to make sacrifices to build a muscular physique. Do not find excuses to skip workouts. Practically, all the top bodybuilders make bodybuilding a main priority. They are not lethargic and they are incredibly devoted.

Positive Mental Attitude

Positive mental attitude does not let you skip your exercise like your meals and motivate you rigorously to move on and on.

Types Of Sets

There are a few different and challenging methods for completing your sets. Let's examine each in detail.

Straight Sets

The oldest style of training and is performed in a direct straight forward manner. In the purest sense, the same weight is used for the same number of sets and reps. The straight-set pattern is probably the best common training technique.

Pyramid Sets

If straight sets are the most common style of training, pyramid sets are closed to it. Instead of using the same weight for the same number of sets and reps, weights are increased with each successive set, while the number of reps is decreased. The pyramid is reached with the heavyweight and fewest number of reps. The weight is then reduced, and the number of reps increased. Primarily, you work your way up one side of the pyramid and down the other.

Factors That Influence Muscle Recovery

The factors that influence muscle recovery includes

Amount Of Damage You Receive

Muscle growth can be considered a compensation process – damaged tissue becomes rebuilt into a slightly bigger, healthier version of itself. As stands to reason, the more damage inflicted, the more time is needed for rebuilding. In general, the more "heavy-duty" your training, the more recovery time you need.

Nutrition

Plan to proper diet plays a huge role in recovery time. Most experts agree that bodybuilders require more food than sedentary individuals. When muscle tissue is being broken down and repaired, significant dietary is needed to aid this process. Besides, an individual needs to recharge his or her glycogen levels between workouts.

Sleep / Rest

Sleep plays a vital role in the recovery process.
Contrary to popular belief, muscles do not grow during the workout. Instead, recovery, and thus growth, takes place after you finish working out, and during sleep in particular. Rest is such a vital component of health that it maximizes your bodybuilding gains if you regularly stay out on a timed pattern. In specific, shorter sessions of sleep throughout the day produce

nearly the same benefits as one longer session. So even a couple of rests will improve your recovery. During sleep, the body breaks down many of the fatigue toxins produced during exercise. It's also said that the most significant release of Testosterone and growth hormone, two of the most potent muscle-building hormones in the body, takes place during sleep.

Tips To Keep You Focused And Motivated

To keep you focused and motivated a few tips are given, they're all easy to implement, free, and practically guaranteed to work!

1. Get a workout partner. There's nothing like a workout partner to push you to stay at your feet. A right training partner knows when to push, focus you on training a little bit harder and when to give you relaxation.

2. For a healthy lifestyle, you may have to add your name to your day planner. The benefit of this is that it helps you balance your workouts with other daily activities that make you keep a healthy lifestyle.

3. Keeping regular pace, don't think that you're going to develop the body in a day or a month or overnight. It may take you years to get into the shape. A few weeks of training will do nothing but make you incredibly stiff and sore, unwilling to work out and to hate the sight of the weights. It's far better to train only three days a week than seven days a week.

4. Rise from the bed and work out! The ultimate question you may want to do early in the morning is to hit the gym. But if you are going during the midday, then keep on trying to build your body. By working out early in the morning you'll be sure of getting it done, you'll feel energized throughout the day.

5. Pick a guru to follow. There's nothing like having someone to look up to you. On days when you don't feel like working out or doing that extra set, ask yourself, what would your role model do?

6. Track of success. Best ways to know where you're going is to understand where you've been, and that is doable when you keep track of your success meter. Start recording things as the amount of cardio, the exercises, the diet, the reps, sets and weight used on each exercise, and how you feel and why.

7. Keep your track of regularity. Missing a workout is not that big a deal. But for many people, keeping track of routine gets complicated because of low motivation or decreasing motivation, but when you keep track of regularity, it keeps you motivated. It is similar to the dieter who eats the entire bag of cookies and a quart of chocolate ice cream. Setbacks and missed workouts are perfectly normal. But the quicker you get back on track, the quicker you will reach your fitness goals.

8. Calculate your progress regularly. If you don't check your progress regularly, you'll be less motivated to push yourself and stay focused. If you're happy with the way you are and just want to maintain a reasonable level of fitness through weights, then that's fine. The chances are that you would like to increase your strength, gain muscle mass, look better and have more energy. Until you calculate your strength, size and cardio levels regularly, you won't feel motivated to push yourself.

9. Get to the gym, get to the gym! We all have days when we just don't want to work out. Force yourself to go to the gym, tell yourself that you will only do the first exercise then will go home. In the early 10 to 15 minutes, you'll start feeling energized and will have a great workout. Sometimes the days when you have the least energy to begin ending up being the days you have your best exercises.

10. Bring change to it. Nothing obliterates motivation and drive like dullness. Keep doing the same routine will leave even the most die-hard fitness radicals tired. That's why you should change your training routine after some time. This change doesn't have to be radical, either, sometimes as simple as increasing or decreasing the number of reps may boost your interest. Try changing the exercises regularly, whatever it takes to get you back on track and focused.

11. Take some time off, but with planning. Earlier, to force
    yourself to the gym, there will be times when taking a few
    days or even a whole week off is suggested. Habitually,
    one of the significant signs of rigorous training, decreases
    the training drive and motivation. In easy terms, your
    body is not getting a chance to recover before the next
    workout fully, and you're undergoing through burnout. It
    is when the beginner weight trainer is most likely to quit
    altogether. If you've been exercising regularly for months,
    if you've tried all the other tips and nothing is helping you
    out, you should get out of your calendar and stop for one
    or two weeks to not train. Write the dates on a scheduler,
    because without registering, taking time off, without a
    plan may turn into undeviating inactivity. Unless you've
    lost concentration in training, a week or two off can have
    you gnawing at the bit to get back to the gym, and if
    training overly was indeed the cause of your motivation
    gap, then you should come back stronger than ever.

Conclusion

Thank you for making it through to the end of *The Plant-Based Vegan Diet for Bodybuilding Athletes*, let's hope it was informative and able to provide you with all of the tools you need to achieve your goals whatever they may be.

The next step is to start making changes in your diet. It's in your hands now. You have the facts about veganism and bodybuilding, and now it is up to you to decide how you are going to make the switch. It's a big switch to make, too, but it is completely doable. I like to suggest that you start with eating vegan two to three times a week and eat the way you are use to the rest of the week, for a month or so. This can help you get used to your new diet and will help your body to adjust.

Then you can increase your vegan days until you are a full-time vegan. That said, if you feel you can jump right into being vegan full-time right off the bat, then do so. Above all else, be easy on yourself. This is a big change, and just like with bodybuilding, you aren't going to be perfect overnight. Take what you have learned in this book and start making healthy changes to your life and diet to improve your bodybuilding.

Finally, if you found this book useful in anyway, a review on Amazon is always appreciated!